THE
GINGER & WHITE
COOKBOOK

THE
GINGER & WHITE
COOKBOOK

Tonia George, Emma Scott & Nicholas Scott

Photography by Jenny Zarins

Mitchell Beazley

THE AUTHORS

Tonia George worked as a food stylist for 10 years and as food editor on the highly acclaimed magazine *Waitrose Food Illustrated*. She is the author of several cookbooks, including *Things on Toast* (she is a self-confessed toast addict) and *A Perfect Start*. Her work has appeared in numerous publications, including *Living etc*, *Red* magazine, US *Food and Wine* and the *Guardian Weekend* magazine.

Nicholas and Emma Scott have forged successful careers in the restaurant and events sector in both London and Sydney. Emma has previously worked at the acclaimed British restaurant St John and Terence Conran's Quaglino's and also catered events including the Wimbledon Tennis Championships. Nick, originally from New Zealand, has worked for some of the top eateries in Sydney, and was astounded by the lack of good coffee shops in London. Together he and Emma ran a consultancy for restaurant owners, which took them all around the world, including to Beijing in the run-up to the Beijing 2008 Olympic Games.

Note: This book contains some dishes made with raw or lightly cooked eggs. It is prudent for more vulnerable people, such as pregnant and nursing mothers, people with weakened immune systems, the elderly, babies and young children to avoid dishes made with uncooked or lightly cooked eggs.

Ginger & White: The Cookbook
by Tonia George, Emma Scott & Nicholas Scott

First published in Great Britain in 2014
by Mitchell Beazley, an imprint of
Octopus Publishing Group Limited,
Endeavour House, 189 Shaftesbury Avenue,
London WC2H 8JY
www.octopusbooks.co.uk

An Hachette UK Company
www.hachette.co.uk

ISBN: 978 1 84533 875 6

Set in Roswell Four and Tribute.

Printed and bound in China.

Photographer: Jenny Zarins
Food Stylist: Tonia George
Props Stylist: Tabitha Hawkins
Illustrator: Abigail Read

Publisher: Alison Starling
Art Director: Jonathan Christie
Senior Art Editor: Juliette Norsworthy
Senior Editor: Leanne Bryan
Assistant Designer: Grace Helmer
Copy Editor: Trish Burgess
Proofreader: Salima Hirani
Indexer: Hilary Bird
Senior Production Manager: Katherine Hockley

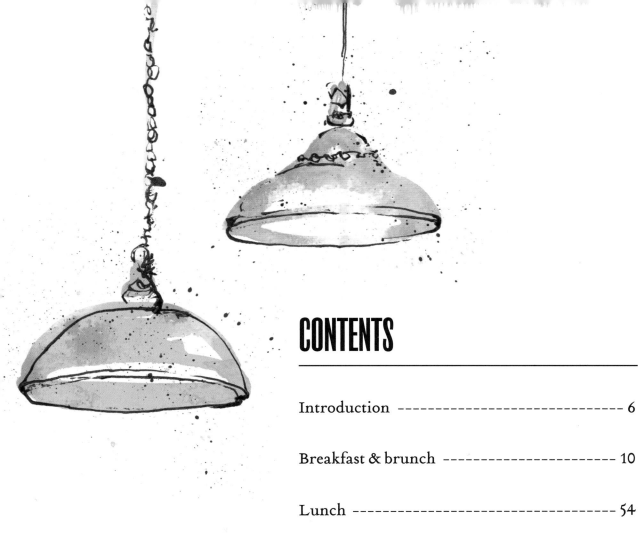

CONTENTS

Introduction

We opened the doors of Ginger & White on a sunny Tuesday in July 2009. It was not the best timing: Emma and Nick were juggling life with a six-month-old baby girl and Tonia was eight months pregnant. Without the budget for an architect, we designed the café ourselves using a ruler and tape measure. We can remember measuring the gap in the counter and toying with how tight we could make it to maximize our minuscule pipsqueak of a kitchen. Then Nick turned to Tonia and ran the tape measure across her bump to check that she could still fit through the gap and that was that: decision made!

This scene pretty much sums up the ad hoc beginnings of Ginger & White. The early days were interspersed with births and babies, but there was also the sad loss of Emma's mum, Jan, a couple of weeks before opening. So although we dutifully crunched the numbers, most of the time we threw out the rulebook and made decisions with our hearts. And one of these was that Ginger & White should have the feel of a family business. There'd be no corporate coffee shop formula for us. Our place would be like an extension of Tonia's kitchen and of Nick and Emma's home, with food lovingly cooked

and shared around a communal dining table, or on a coffee table in front of a comfy leather sofa. This was to be a place for sharing food, conversation and laughter.

In our opinion, the café scene in London was in a sorry state and a long way behind that of New Zealand and Australia. It consisted mainly of American-style coffee chains pumping out what they called 'real coffee expertly made by baristas', but that we thought would be better described as 'frothy pints of milky nothingness'. Our coffee was definitely real, but how could we describe it in a way that distinguished it from the chain-produced product? We eventually came up with, 'We *don't* do Grande!' which we hoped would tell our customers that we took coffee seriously enough not to drown it in lukewarm milk.

We talked and talked for months about the perfect café, stitching together the best bits from the antipodean café scene, but desperately wanting to keep a flavour of the traditional British 'caff'. So we stood by classics such as the bacon buttie and baked beans on toast, though our beans were braised with smoked paprika and sweetened with

muscovado sugar instead of being poured from a tin. Similarly, the bacon we used came from free-range Blythburgh pigs and the ketchup was a spicy number from Wiltshire. We knew that using artisan produce from farmers' markets was going to reduce our profit margin, but we couldn't bring ourselves to go down the well-trodden road of using big, faceless and much cheaper catering suppliers.

Having decided on the ethos of our café, we now needed to find the perfect corner of London for it. Easier said than done. We looked at countless potential sites, many of which were soulless. One kebab shop had a basement of bunk beds and more people than you would think could possibly fit in it. And then we came across Chaiwalla, a little chai shop tucked down a pedestrianized side street in leafy Hampstead. The locals had not quite taken to the idea of drinking chai from terracotta cups whilst perching on Bollywood-style pouffes and then smashing the cups outside, so the owner was selling up. We knew it was perfect for us straight away.

Once up and running, Ginger & White was quickly packed with customers who all

became part of the family. From tiny tots to octogenarians, everyone loved dunking toast soldiers into soft-boiled eggs decorated with little woolly hats.

And it is to all our wonderful customers, who have taken us into their hearts, that we dedicate this book; and to our loyal staff, who often feel to us like an excited brood of teenage offspring; and, of course, to our own little munchkins, who are always willing and eager to help when cakes need tasting. Thank you also to the grandmas who have knitted our egg cosies or shared trusted family recipes,

and to our littlest customers, whom we have nurtured with many a babyccino, fish finger sarnie and dippy egg.

We want to share this collection of recipes with the entire extended Ginger & White family. Unlike some cheffy cookbooks that need tweaking to be usable in the domestic kitchen, this one consists of dishes that can genuinely be made at home – all the way from our homes to yours – to give you loads of enjoyment with lashings of laughter and fun.

Breakfast & brunch

How to make great coffee

Making great coffee is almost a culinary art. The secret, of course, is to start with great ingredients. At G&W we use freshly roasted beans that are bagged and then stored for 7–10 days before opening. After that, we grind only what is needed, and recommend you do the same, whether it's for an espresso machine, a stove-top percolator or a drip filter.

1. Getting the beans

There are two ways to get your hands on great beans: walk into your nearest independent coffee shop, which may actually roast on the premises, or go online and subscribe to one of the boutique roasters. Top of our list is Square Mile Coffee Roasters, whom we've used since day one. However, other notable suppliers include Carvetii, Climpson & Sons, Caravan, Volcano Coffee Works and Ozone.

2. Grinding the beans

If you are lucky enough to have an espresso machine at home, you will need to grind your beans very finely. They should be a little coarser for a stove-top pot, and quite coarse for a cafetière or drip filter. There are excellent hand grinders now available, or you can splash out on an electric grinder, but try to avoid using a spice grinder as they give very uneven results.

3. Tamping

Let's assume you have an espresso machine: place freshly ground coffee in the basket of your portafilter then tamp firmly and evenly (preferably with a tamper) until the coffee pushes back. This produces a firm 'puck' of grounds for extraction. A nicely weighted tamper feels great in the hand and is worth the investment.

4. Pulling the shot

A good double espresso (about 30ml) should take 27–30 seconds to extract. Any longer and the coffee might taste watery and sour; any less and the coffee will be missing all the wonderful caramel and fruity notes you'd expect to find in a perfectly pulled shot.

5. The milk

The success of your coffee now rests on nailing the creamy, velvety milk. Take a stainless steel jug, wider at the bottom than at the top, and half-fill it with cold, fresh whole milk.

Blast the steam wand into a tea towel to purge any water built up in the pipes, then insert the wand into the milk. Turn on the steam and bring the nozzle to the surface until you hear air being sucked into the milk. It should make a gentle phsh, phsh sound rather than a loud sucking noise. Do this for just a few seconds, then submerge the wand and tilt the jug slightly to create a whirlpool effect that produces microfoam – milk like silk. It's important not to suck too much air into the milk in those first few seconds as it will create big bubbles that are difficult to get rid of.

When your hand can no longer stand the heat from the bottom of the jug, the milk is hot enough and ready to pour. Tap the jug on the counter top to help knock out any large bubbles that have snuck in, then 'back-blend' (swirl) the milk to keep it silky and smooth.

6. The pour

With your jug held high, start pouring the milk, dropping closer to the cup to create latte art patterns on top of the finished drink.

Relax and enjoy!

Coffee types

Coffee was always going to be one of the cornerstones of Ginger & White. And while the London coffee scene has come of age in recent times, with many different brewing methods on offer, we choose to concentrate on the union of humble espresso and milk like silk. Ever true to our motto 'We *don't* do Grande!' we're proud to think that, over the years, we've helped steer Londoners towards smaller, stronger and, ultimately, tastier coffee.

ESPRESSO – about 25ml extracted in 27–30 seconds, this is where the perfect coffee begins; concentrating all the aromas and flavours of the bean into a smooth, golden liquid.

MACCHIATO – an espresso shot just 'stained' with hot milk to take the edge off.

CORTADO – a single espresso combined with an equal amount of creamy milk; it's a smaller version of a flat white.

LONG BLACK – a double espresso with a touch more water.

CAPPUCCINO – a double espresso topped with plenty of velvety microfoam; this is the strongest of the milky coffees, traditionally drunk at breakfast.

FLAT WHITE – a double espresso combined with an equal amount of creamy milk, somewhere between a cappuccino and a caffe latte; antipodean in origin.

CAFFE LATTE – a single espresso with creamy milk in a 225ml glass; the milkiest coffee of them all.

Banana & wheatgerm smoothie

The perfect bananas for this recipe should be yellow with just a few brown spots. Slice and freeze them before use so that the smoothie is beautifully chilled with no need to add ice. This will keep it thick and luscious.

Place all the ingredients in a blender and blitz for 30–45 seconds, until smooth. Serve immediately.

SERVES 1

6 pieces of frozen banana (about 120g)

50ml natural yogurt

100ml milk

1 tsp honey

1 scant tsp wheatgerm

Grapefruit & orange morning juice

Mixing a dash of freshly squeezed mouth-puckering grapefruit into your morning OJ gives it a really tangy edge. It feels more cleansing and better for you than just sweet orange juice and is packed full of vitamin C. Look out for navel oranges, which yield lots more juice than regular ones.

Squeeze the juice out of the grapefruit and the oranges. Pour into a glass filled with ice and serve immediately.

SERVES 1

1 grapefruit, halved

3 oranges, halved

ice

Bloody Mary

It's very easy to throw together an average Bloody Mary, but for a drink that makes your tastebuds tingle, every ingredient needs to earn its place. We found our sweet spot with a clean, crisp vodka from Suffolk, which we layer with just the right amount of tomato juice spiked with the classic condiments. Be warned: it is seriously spicy.

Sprinkle some celery salt on to a saucer. Run the lemon wedge around the rim of a glass, then dip the rim in the celery salt.

Fill the glass with ice and add the vodka. Squeeze the lemon into it, then add the wedge to the glass. Add the tomato juice, plus a dash of Tabasco and Worcestershire sauce, then stir and taste. Adjust the spice level by adding more sauce as necessary.

Garnish the drink with the cucumber or celery stick, then add a twist of black pepper on top.

SERVES 1

celery salt

lemon wedge

ice

50ml clean, crisp vodka, such as Adnams Suffolk Barley Vodka

100ml tomato juice

Tabasco sauce

Worcestershire sauce

cucumber slice or celery stick, to garnish

freshly ground black pepper

Blood orange buck's fizz

We're bordering on obsessed with the darkly crimson blood orange. It adds a splash of vivid colour to a wintry brunch table and its juice is an excellent addition to a lunchtime glass of bubbly, such as Chapeldown Vintage Reserve. Made in Kent using the same grapes and method as champagne, it's a wonderful example of great British produce.

Juice the blood oranges into a jug.

Pour the juice into 8–10 champagne flutes, depending on size, until they are about one-third full. Top up with the sparkling wine.

SERVES 8–10

10 blood oranges, halved

750ml bottle of chilled sparkling wine, such as Chapeldown Vintage Reserve

Hot chocolate
with marshmallows

We use luxurious Montezuma's chocolate, which, when mixed with creamy milk, is pretty much the eighth wonder of the world. Just ask Wendy, our resident hot chocolate connoisseur, who you'll find in our Hampstead branch on any given day. To spice things up a bit, try using chocolate flavoured with mint, chilli or bitter orange.

Put the chocolate and cocoa into an enamel mug. Add the water and stir to make a paste.

Steam the milk, stretching it with your steam wand, or heat on the hob to just below boiling point. Whisk it into the chocolate paste, then float the marshmallows on top and serve straight away.

SERVES 1

2 heaped tbsp grated dark chocolate (at least 70 per cent cocoa solids)

1 heaped tbsp cocoa powder

1 tbsp boiling water

200ml whole milk

2 big marshmallows or a handful of mini ones

Toasted banana bread
with vanilla cream cheese, rhubarb & raspberries

Here's another weekend favourite – one of the prettiest brunch dishes. When young, Barbie-pink rhubarb is in season, we roast it in the oven with just a shake of sugar so that it keeps its colour and shape. The sharpness of this topping goes brilliantly with the warm and spicy banana bread, which is another of our guilty pleasures.

Preheat the oven to 180°C/fan 160°C/gas mark 4. Grease a 900g loaf tin and base-line with nonstick baking paper.

Cream the butter and sugar in a bowl until pale and fluffy. Beat in about a quarter of the eggs at a time.

In another bowl, mash the bananas with a fork and stir in the vanilla extract. Mix into the creamed butter, then fold in all the remaining dry ingredients. Finally, stir in the buttermilk until you have a smooth batter.

Pour the mixture into the prepared tin, using a flexible spatula to get every last bit from the bowl, and bake on the middle shelf for 30–40 minutes, until a skewer inserted in the centre comes out clean. Remove the bread from the oven and leave to cool in the tin, but leave the oven on.

Now prepare the rhubarb. Put the vanilla sugar into a baking dish, toss the rhubarb in it and bake for 15 minutes, until just tender. Allow to cool.

Preheat the grill on a medium setting.

Meanwhile, make the vanilla cream cheese by beating the cream cheese, yogurt and vanilla bean paste together until smooth. Sift in the icing sugar and beat again.

Toast 4 thick slices of the banana bread under the grill on both sides. Watch them carefully because they can quickly blacken around the edges.

To serve, top each slice with a dollop of vanilla cream cheese, 3–4 rhubarb pieces and a scattering of raspberries. Finish with a drizzle of honey and serve.

SERVES 4

125g unsalted butter, softened, plus extra for greasing

325g golden caster sugar

2 free-range eggs, beaten

3 very ripe bananas

¼ tsp vanilla extract

250g plain flour

1 tsp bicarbonate of soda

½ tsp fine salt

½ tsp ground cinnamon

generous pinch of ground allspice

120ml buttermilk

1 punnet raspberries

75g clear honey

For the rhubarb

2 tbsp vanilla sugar

300g pink forced rhubarb, cut into 7.5cm lengths

For the vanilla cream cheese

200g cream cheese

75g plain yogurt

⅛ tsp vanilla bean paste

2 tbsp icing sugar

Spiced plum & almond eggy bread

For this recipe we soak slices of day-old bloomer in plenty of cream, eggs and milk and fry them until crisp and golden. We then pile them high with roasted British plums, which reach their best at the tail end of summer. Be sure not to overcook them or they'll go mushy and lose their shape. In early summer we use berries rather than plums; and once the plum season has passed, we use bananas.

Preheat the oven to 200°C/fan 180°C/gas mark 6.

Place the plums in a baking dish and sprinkle with the muscovado sugar, spices and water. Cover with foil and roast for 25 minutes, until the fruit is soft but still holding its shape. Leave the oven on.

Meanwhile, put the eggs, cream, milk, vanilla paste and caster sugar into a bowl and beat them together. Add the bread, turn to coat thoroughly and leave to soak for 30 minutes.

When the plums are ready, set them aside at room temperature for the syrup to thicken, or drain the syrup into a saucepan and reduce it over a medium heat until it has thickened.

Heat the sunflower oil in a frying pan and fry the eggy bread on each side until crisp (you may need to do this in batches). Transfer the bread to a baking sheet and place in the hot oven for 2–3 minutes, until puffed up.

Cut the bread in half diagonally and place on 2 plates. Top each piece with with the roasted plum halves and drizzle the syrup all over. Sprinkle with flaked almonds, if desired, and serve immediately.

SERVES 2

| 4 red plums, halved and stoned |
| 15g light muscovado sugar |
| pinch of ground cinnamon |
| 1 star anise |
| 1 tbsp water |
| 2 free-range eggs |
| 1 tbsp double cream |
| 2 tbsp milk |
| smear of vanilla paste |
| 15g caster sugar |
| 2 thick crustless slices of white farmhouse bread, preferably 1 day old |
| 50ml sunflower oil |
| 15g toasted flaked almonds, to garnish (optional) |

Nutty honey granola
with berry & spice compote

Similar to muesli, granola is easy to make and keeps for a month. The trick is getting it to bake to a crisp texture without creating any bitter flavours, which is what happens if you overdo it. Texture and colour are not good checks for readiness because the mixture will feel soft until it completely cools. Our teacup test will help you to judge it accurately.

Preheat the oven to 160°C/fan 140°C/gas mark 3.

Place the honey, sugar, oil and cinnamon in a small saucepan over a low heat and warm, without stirring, until the sugar has dissolved.

Put the oats, nuts, seeds and salt into a large bowl. Pour in the hot sugary mixture and stir well.

Tip the granola into 2 large roasting trays, making a layer no more than 3cm deep. Bake for 25–35 minutes, then stir to swap the position of the darker oats at the edges with the lighter oats in the middle. Bake for another 20–30 minutes, until pale golden. To check it is done, put a spoonful of the granola into a teacup and rattle it around until completely cool. If it makes a clattery sound against the china, it is crunchy enough. If not, bake for a little longer.

Allow the mixture to cool for 10 minutes before stirring in the cranberries, sultanas or dried fruit, then set aside to cool completely. Store in an airtight container for up to 1 month.

We serve the granola with thick yogurt drizzled with honey, a dollop of our berry and spice compote, and a spoonful of berries, if they are in season.

MAKES 1KG

250g clear honey

125g caster sugar

60ml sunflower oil

1 tsp ground cinnamon

400g jumbo oats

50g flaked almonds

50g walnuts, roughly chopped

100g sunflower seeds

50g pumpkin seeds

100g sesame seeds

½ tsp table salt

100g dried cranberries, golden sultanas, dried bananas or any chopped dried fruit

To serve

thick natural or Greek yogurt

clear honey

Berry & Spice Compote (*see* page 157)

fresh berries (optional)

Fruity crumble muffins

Every morning our shops are filled with the sweet scent of buttery crumble muffins. Baking these is the first job of the day so that we can have them ready for our first customers on their way to work. Originally, we studded them with seasonal fruit, but our chefs have since come up with so many flavours that we could probably dedicate a whole book to them. The nutty crumble topping gives them a great British twist. To ring the changes, try replacing the fruit according to the variations opposite.

Preheat the oven to 180°C/fan 160°C/gas mark 4. Line a 6-hole muffin tin with paper cases, or set out a silicone muffin tray.

Put the butter into a glass jug and heat in the microwave until melted. Add the buttermilk, then whisk in the egg.

Combine all the dry ingredients (except the fruit) in a bowl and add the egg mixture, stirring until there are no floury pockets (it can be a bit lumpy). Fold in the fruit, then spoon the mixture into the paper cases or muffin tray, almost to the top of each hole.

To make the crumble topping, place the flour and butter in a bowl and rub together until the mixture resembles coarse clumpy breadcrumbs. Stir in the sugar and nuts.

Pile a good 2 tablespoons of the crumble mixture on to each muffin and bake for 25–30 minutes. Turn out of the tin or tray and place upside down to cool (the muffins are top heavy, so doing this prevents the lighter sponge underneath from getting squished).

MAKES 6

60g unsalted butter

150ml buttermilk

1 free-range egg

200g plain flour

1 tsp baking powder

¼ tsp bicarbonate of soda

75g caster sugar

pinch of salt

100g chopped fresh fruit

For the crumble topping

60g plain flour

45g chilled butter, cubed

20g caster sugar

50g almonds, walnuts or pine nuts, chopped

VARIATIONS

Rhubarb, vanilla & almond muffins:
Thinly slice 2 sticks of tender forced
rhubarb and add to the muffin batter
along with ¼ tsp vanilla paste. Use
flaked almonds in the crumble topping
instead of chopped. Bake as opposite.

Apple, cinnamon & walnut muffins:
Peel and core 2 Granny Smith apples,
then coarsely grate them into the
muffin batter. Add 1 tsp cinnamon
to the crumble topping and choose
chopped walnuts. Bake as opposite.

Chocolate swirl muffins:
Mix 50g cocoa powder with 15ml
boiling water until smooth, then
lightly swirl into the muffin batter
to create a marbled effect. Stir in
50g white chocolate chips and grate
some dark chocolate on top instead of
using the crumble topping. Bake
as opposite.

Mixed berry muffins:
Add 75g raspberries and/or
blueberries to the batter. Omit the
crumble and scatter a few more berries
on top so they burst during baking and
give a sneak preview of what's inside.

Roasted peanut butter

Our peanut butter is legendary in certain parts of northwest London. Such is its popularity that we're a little scared to part with this recipe in case our customers desert us. It is crazily simple: you just need to be brave enough to roast the nuts to a good golden colour and have a flair for balancing sweet with salt. Unlike jam, peanut butter is not boiled, so it must always be kept refrigerated and eaten within 6 weeks.

Preheat the oven to 180°C/fan 160°C/gas mark 4. Sterilize your jars and lids (*see* tip, below).

Place the peanuts in a large roasting tin and roast until golden (35–45 minutes), stirring if they start to brown unevenly. The skins will peel open to reveal a developing tan underneath. When the peanuts are deeply bronzed, as though just back from the Caribbean, they are ready.

Transfer the nuts, still in their skins, to a blender or food processor. Add the remaining ingredients and blitz until combined.

Scrape down the sides of the blender or bowl with a spatula and blend again. You need a textured but spreadable paste, so add more oil if it feels too stiff. Taste and add more salt or sugar as you prefer. Using a spatula, transfer the mixture to your sterilized jars. Seal tightly, then label and date.

MAKES 700G

500g unsalted peanuts, with skin
1 tsp sea salt
175ml groundnut oil
1 tbsp clear honey
1 tbsp demerara sugar

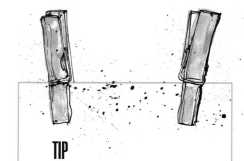

TIP

It's important to wash and sterilize both jars and lids before storing preserves in them so that they are free of bacteria that could taint the content. We wash ours in the dishwasher, then place them upside down in a low oven for 30 minutes to ensure they are thoroughly dry.

Spicy baked beans
with red peppers, chorizo & feta

Our famous baked beans have been on the menu since the day we first opened our doors in Hampstead and they epitomize our playful approach to food. Beans have always been a guilty pleasure of ours, so we gave them an adult twist, balancing the sweetness with a sour tang and spiking them with chilli. In their latest makeover we top them with fried slices of Bath pig chorizo and salty feta, so we're more in love with them now than ever. They're always the first thing that Tonia and Emma order when they're in the café.

Drain the beans, transfer them to a saucepan and cover with plenty of water (do not add salt). Bring to the boil, then cover, reduce the heat and simmer for 45 minutes, until tender. Drain again.

Meanwhile, heat the butter in a large flameproof casserole dish and fry the onions and peppers until the onion is very soft and sweet, but not coloured. Cover the dish and cook over a low heat for 30 minutes, stirring now and then.

When the onion mixture is soft and sticky, add the mustard powder, paprika, chilli, molasses or sugar, tomatoes, boiling water and vinegar. Add the beans, cover with a lid and simmer over a low heat for 1 hour. Season with the salt, stir well and taste. If too sweet, add more salt and 2–3 tablespoons more vinegar. If too dry, add a little more boiling water. If too runny, cook uncovered until the sauce has thickened a little. It will thicken more on cooling.

To make the topping, place the chorizo in a heavy-based pan and fry until crisp.

Reheat the beans and serve them in a bowl topped with the fried chorizo, crumbled feta and a sprinkling of parsley. Serve with buttered toast on the side.

SERVES 4

400g dried mixed beans, such as haricot beans, butter beans and chickpeas, soaked overnight in 3 times their depth of water

50g butter

2 red onions, thickly sliced

2 red peppers, deseeded and thickly sliced

1 tsp English mustard powder

1 tsp smoked sweet paprika

½ tsp dried chilli flakes

50g molasses or dark muscovado sugar

400g can plum tomatoes

500ml boiling water

4 tbsp cider vinegar

2 tsp salt

buttered sourdough or granary toast, to serve

For the topping

200g chunky chorizo, sliced

50g feta cheese, crumbled

2 sprigs flat-leaf parsley, leaves picked and roughly chopped

Sweetcorn fritters
with chilli jam & slow-roasted tomatoes

Although this is a typically Aussie brunch dish, we felt it deserved a place on our menu because we all adore it. We sell a lot of these fritters at weekends, often with our amazing Blythburgh bacon and, when avocados are nutty and creamy, we mash them up with lime juice and use them in place of the crème fraîche.

Place the flour, bicarbonate of soda, polenta and cayenne pepper in a mixing bowl.

In a separate bowl whisk together the eggs and yogurt. Mix in the sweetcorn and spring onions, then pour the mixture into the flour and stir until combined. Season well with salt and pepper. The batter should have a fairly firm consistency.

Heat 1 tablespoon oil in a frying pan over a low–medium heat, then drop 3 tablespoons of the batter into the pan to create 3 small fritters. Cook for 4–6 minutes, turning halfway through, until thoroughly cooked and golden on both sides. Repeat with the remaining batter, keeping the cooked fritters warm.

Serve each person 3 fritters with 2 slow-roasted tomato halves, 2 rashers of bacon, a dollop of crème fraîche and a blob of chilli jam. Garnish with the rocket leaves.

SERVES 4

75g self-raising flour

½ tsp bicarbonate of soda

50g polenta

pinch of cayenne pepper

2 free-range eggs

150ml Greek yogurt

400g (drained weight) canned or frozen sweetcorn, defrosted if frozen

6 spring onions, trimmed and sliced

½ tsp salt

freshly ground black pepper

sunflower oil, for frying

To serve

4 Slow-roasted Tomatoes (*see* page 148)

8 rashers of bacon, fried

100g crème fraîche

4 tbsp chilli jam

rocket leaves

Four types of mini frittata

EACH RECIPE MAKES 4–6

Adding cream to the eggs in these recipes gives the frittatas a smoother texture and stabilizes them. It's also totally delicious and just a tiny bit naughty. We like to bake them in 4-hole Yorkshire pudding tins, but you could use muffin tins instead – being deeper, they might take about 5 minutes longer to bake. Serve with a sharply dressed salad for a light lunch.

Cheddar, thyme & caramelized onion

Preheat the oven to 200°C/fan 180°C/gas mark 6. Drizzle 1 teaspoon olive oil into the holes in your baking tin(s).

Place the butter, onions and thyme in a small saucepan. Cover and cook over a very low heat for 15 minutes, until the onion is caramelized. Add the garlic and cook for another 2 minutes.

Meanwhile, put the eggs, yolks, cream and cheese into a bowl and beat together. Add the onion mixture, then spoon into the prepared baking tin(s). Place on a baking sheet and bake for 25–30 minutes, until golden and not too wobbly in the middle. Cool in the tin, then serve.

olive oil, for greasing

15g butter

2 onions, sliced

few sprigs of thyme

2 garlic cloves, chopped

6 free-range eggs plus 2 yolks

600ml double cream

125g mature Cheddar cheese, grated

Chorizo & pepper

Preheat the oven to 200°C/fan 180°C/gas mark 6. Drizzle 1 teaspoon olive oil into the holes in your baking tin(s).

Put the eggs, yolk and cream into a bowl, add salt and pepper and beat together. Add the thyme, peppers and half the chorizo. Divide between the prepared holes in the baking tins. Top with the remaining chorizo and season with salt and pepper.

Place on a baking sheet and bake for 25–30 minutes, until golden around the edges and not too wobbly in the middle. Cool in the tin, then serve.

olive oil, for greasing

6 free-range eggs plus 1 yolk

500ml double cream

few sprigs of thyme

100g roasted red peppers in oil, drained and sliced

200g chorizo, sliced

salt and pepper

Feta, tomato & spinach

Preheat the oven to 200°C/fan 180°C/gas mark 6. Drizzle 1 teaspoon olive oil into the holes in your baking tin(s).

Place the spinach in a large saucepan with 1 tablespoon olive oil, cover and heat until wilted. Drain and chop.

Put the eggs, yolk and cream into a bowl, add salt and pepper and beat together.

Combine the spinach with the egg mixture and half the feta. Divide between the prepared holes in the baking tins. Top with the remaining feta and the slow-roasted tomatoes, drizzle with oil and season with salt and pepper. Place on a baking sheet and bake for 25–30 minutes, until golden around the edges and not too wobbly in the middle. Cool in the tin, then serve.

1 tbsp olive oil, plus extra for greasing

400g baby spinach

5 free-range eggs plus 1 yolk

500ml double cream

200g feta cheese, cubed or crumbled

6 halves of Slow-roasted Tomatoes (*see* page 148)

salt and pepper

Salmon, onion & anchovy

Preheat the oven to 200°C/fan 180°C/gas mark 6. Drizzle 1 teaspoon olive oil into the holes in your baking tin(s).

Put the eggs, yolks, cream and herbs into a bowl and beat together.

Divide the smoked salmon, spring onions and anchovies between the prepared holes in the baking tins. Top up with the egg mixture and place on a baking sheet. Bake for 25–30 minutes, until golden around the edges and not too wobbly in the middle. Cool in the tin, then serve.

olive oil, for greasing

6 free-range eggs plus 2 yolks

600ml double cream

3 tbsp chopped herbs, such as dill, parsley and/or chives

150g hot-smoked salmon fillet or smoked salmon, chopped

6 spring onions, sliced

6 anchovy fillets, chopped

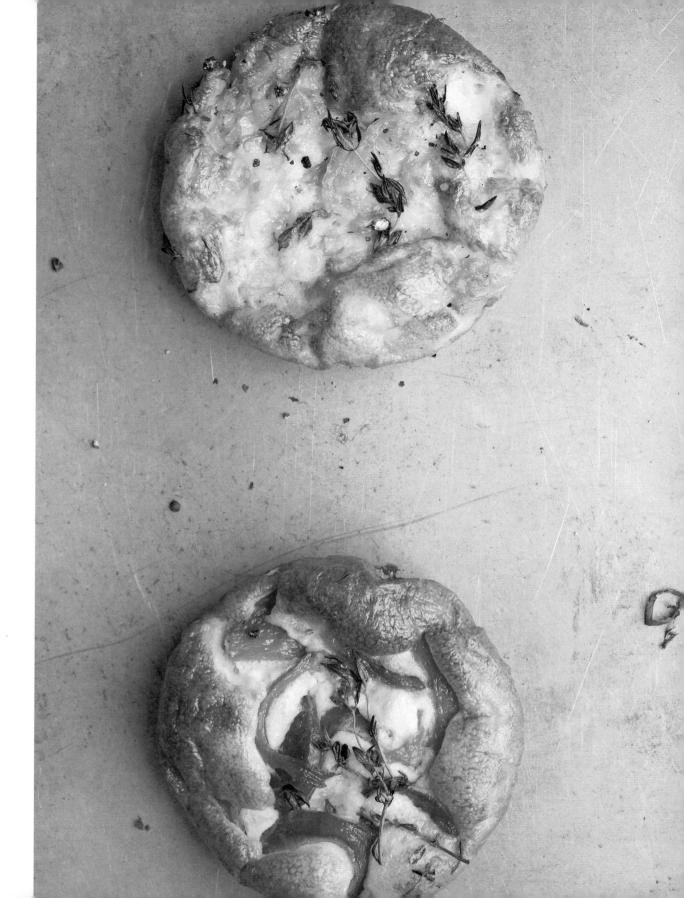

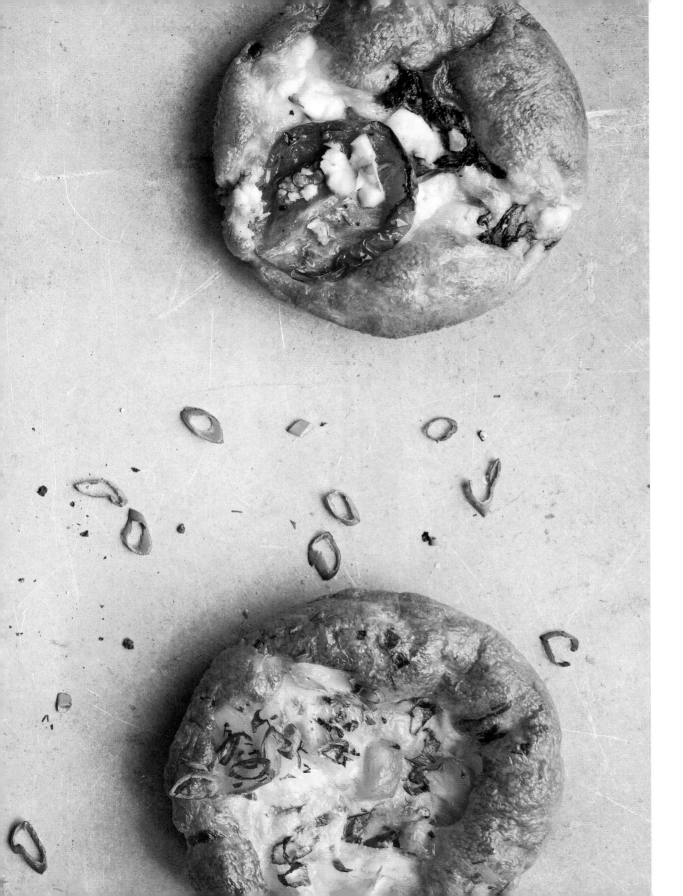

Fried duck eggs
with black pudding & sourdough croutons

We love the pear, date and ale chutney that one of our suppliers makes for us, but you can use any fruity relish to accompany this dish, or replace it with traditional British brown sauce. We use the fairytale white eggs that ducks lay in the daylight hours of spring and summer; they tend to be larger than hen's eggs, so need a little bit longer when frying.

Warm 4 plates. Heat 1 tablespoon of the olive oil in a large frying pan and fry the black pudding over a medium heat until crisp.

Add the croutons and heat for a few minutes to warm through and combine with the other flavours. Tip into a bowl, cover with foil and keep warm.

Wipe out the pan, add 2 tablespoons of the olive oil and place over a high heat. When hot, crack 4 of the eggs into the pan, cover with a lid and cook for 1–2 minutes, until the whites are set but the yolks are molten. Transfer to 2 warm plates and keep warm. Cook the remaining eggs in the same way and put them on the remaining warm plates.

Dust all the eggs with the chilli flakes, scatter the crouton and black pudding mixture over them then dollop a spoonful of the relish on to each plate. Garnish with parsley and serve straight away.

SERVES 4

5 tbsp olive oil

300g black pudding, roughly chopped

100g Rosemary Sourdough Croutons (*see* page 155)

8 free-range eggs

¼ tsp chilli flakes

6 tbsp fruity relish, such as England Preserves's Pear, Date and Ale Chutney

4 tbsp roughly chopped flat-leaf parsley leaves, to garnish

Soft-boiled eggs
with toast soldiers

The very precise way in which we cook our boiled eggs sums up our attitude to food: they have to be perfect every time. Tonia's mum, who used to keep chickens, came up with this great way of cooking perfect boiled eggs. Instead of doing them at a rolling boil, which can make them tough, she rests them in hot water, which coaxes them into a creamy set white with a molten golden yolk. Topped with little woolly hats to keep them warm, what could be better?

Bring a medium saucepan of water to the boil. Turn the heat down to the gentlest simmer and lower the eggs into the water using a slotted spoon. Boil for 1 minute, then take off the heat, cover with a lid and set aside for 4 minutes (use a timer for this).

Toast the bread, then butter it and slice it into soldiers about 2cm thick.

Put 4 egg cups on 2 small plates with a teaspoon and the soldiers. When the timer goes, make sure you're ready to sit down, as the eggs need to be cracked and eaten immediately. Offer Marmite and Gentleman's Relish alongside, if liked.

SERVES 2

4 free-range eggs, at room temperature

4 thick slices of white bread, from a tin loaf

salted butter, softened

Marmite or Gentleman's Relish, to serve (optional)

Chorizo & slow-roasted tomato omelette

This is one of the simplest and tastiest recipes in the book. As unashamed toast addicts, we serve a lot of our breakfast dishes on toast, but this one is completely gluten-free. A scattering of Rosemary Sourdough Croutons (*see* page 155) or a drizzle of garlicky yogurt can elevate the humble omelette into something sublime.

Place a dry, heavy-based frying pan over a high heat. When hot, cook the chorizo for a minute on each side until crisp. Transfer to a plate.

Add the olive oil to the hot pan, then pour in the beaten eggs. Season and cook, tilting the pan so that the omelette sets in a thin layer, almost like a pancake.

Add the slow-roasted tomatoes and reserved chorizo and cook until just set on top. Sprinkle with the parsley.

Using a large fish slice or palette knife, lift or slide the open omelette onto a plate and serve immediately.

SERVES 1

50g chorizo, thinly sliced

1 tbsp olive oil

2 free-range eggs, beaten

salt and pepper

5 halves of Slow-roasted Tomatoes (*see* page 148)

handful of flat-leaf parsley, leaves picked

Scrambled eggs
with buttermilk & smoked salmon

Our secret is out: we add buttermilk to scrambled eggs. This gives them a lighter texture than when adding cream, but a slightly different (almost cheesy) texture than when adding milk. It's important not to have the heat too high, or the eggs can quickly overcook. Also, take them off the heat while they are still a little runny on top and they will finish cooking in the warmth of the pan. Another trick is to have your toast ready and waiting so you can take the eggs out of the pan the moment they are cooked to perfection. Egg cookery is all about precision and being a pedant really helps!

Crack the eggs into a bowl, add the buttermilk and seasoning, then whisk until just blended – don't overbeat them.

Put the bread in the toaster, get your plates and cutlery ready and have some softened butter to hand.

Heat a frying pan over a medium heat and melt the butter. Turn the heat as low as possible, then pour in the eggs and let them almost set underneath. Using a spatula, fold them into the centre – don't break them up too vigorously or you'll get a weird bitty texture. When the eggs are still runny on top, remove them from the heat and continue to fold them so they are only just cooked through.

Quickly butter your toast and pile the eggs on it. Fold the salmon over the eggs and finish with chopped chives, then add a twist of black pepper on top.

SERVES 2

6 free-range eggs

60ml buttermilk

salt and pepper

4 slices of sourdough bread

20g butter, plus extra for spreading

150g smoked salmon

chopped chives, to garnish

Chorizo, avocado & lime on toast

There are few dishes that are not improved by the intense smoky flavour of chorizo. We slice and fry it lightly until it is crisp and the paprika-stained juices are released. When avocados are at their peak, their flesh should be creamy with a slightly nutty edge, but in our opinion they need to be perked up a bit with a shake of Tabasco, a squeeze of lime and a tickle of salt just to tease out their flavour.

Put the avocado flesh into a bowl, add the lime juice and roughly mash together. Add a shake of Tabasco, a good twist of black pepper and the salt. Cover with clingfilm to prevent the flesh turning brown.

Place a dry, heavy-based frying pan over a high heat. When hot, briefly fry the chorizo on both sides until it releases its fat.

Heat a griddle pan until very hot. Add the ciabatta and toast on both sides.

Spread the avocado mixture on the toast, top with a few slices of warm chorizo, some slow-roasted tomatoes, rocket leaves and a drizzle of olive oil.

SERVES 4

2 ripe avocados, halved and stoned

juice of ½ lime

Tabasco sauce

freshly ground black pepper

½ tsp sea salt

200g chorizo, thinly sliced in extreme diagonals (almost horizontal)

1 ciabatta loaf, cut in half horizontally and then into 4 widthways

12 pieces of Slow-roasted Tomatoes (*see* page 148)

handful of rocket leaves

extra virgin olive oil, for drizzling

Portobello mushrooms
with roasted garlic mayo on potato sourdough

Roasting mushrooms really brings out their earthy flavour, providing a satisfying alternative to meat for vegetarians. We serve them on a thickly crusted, chewy sourdough made with potatoes, which provides a good contrast to their soft texture. If you don't have time to make the Roasted Garlic Mayonnaise, simply crush a quarter of a garlic clove and stir it into some mayo or, even easier, rub the toast with a cut garlic clove instead.

Preheat the oven to 200°C/fan 180°C/gas mark 6.

Clean the mushrooms, discarding the stalks. Place them in a roasting tin, drizzle with the olive oil and season with salt and pepper.

Roast the mushrooms for 15 minutes, until softened. Turn them over and roast for a further 10 minutes.

Toast the sourdough on both sides, then spread the garlic mayo on the toast and divide it between 2 plates. Top each slice with a mushroom.

Dress the rocket in olive oil with a little salt and pepper. Pile on top of the mushrooms and serve.

SERVES 2

4 Portobello mushrooms

1 tbsp extra virgin olive oil, plus extra for dressing

salt and pepper

4 thick slices of potato sourdough

4 tbsp Roasted Garlic Mayonnaise (*see* page 150)

handful of rocket leaves

Kedgeree

At weekends we serve kedgeree for breakfast, as is traditional, but we also serve it for supper because we just adore it. A good kedgeree has all the components cooked to perfection and lightly combined so they don't break up too much. Ours is a buttery number with fluffy grains of lightly spiced rice and plump pieces of smoky fish, finished off with eggs that are just runny in the centre.

Melt 50g of the butter in a saucepan over a low heat. Add the onions, cover with a lid and cook for 10 minutes, until soft and translucent.

Meanwhile, simmer the eggs for 4 minutes, but allow them to sit in the hot water for 6 minutes. Drain, then run cold water over them until cool. Peel and halve, then set aside.

Place the rice in a saucepan with the water, bay leaves and salt. Bring to the boil, clamp on a lid and simmer on the lowest possible heat for 5 minutes. Set aside, keeping the lid on. By the time you're ready to use it, the water will have been absorbed and the grains will be fluffy.

Add the spices to the onion and cook for 2 minutes, until they are golden brown.

Place the smoked haddock in a pan, skin side down, and pour in the milk. Simmer very gently for 3–4 minutes, until the thickest part has lost its transparency. Drain, remove the skin and bones, and flake into large chunks.

Heat the remaining butter in a large frying pan and add the cooked rice and spiced onions. Fold in the flaked haddock, being careful not to break it up too much. Top with the halved boiled eggs. (The kedgeree can be served straight from the pan or arranged on individual plates.)

Serve with the lemon wedges, a scattering of coriander leaves and a good twist of black pepper, and offer mango chutney and natural yogurt in separate bowls for people to help themselves.

SERVES 4

125g butter

2 large onions, thinly sliced

4 free-range eggs

175g Basmati rice, washed several times until the water is clear

250ml cold water

2 bay leaves

½ tsp salt

1 tbsp mild curry powder

5 cardamom pods, crushed

600g undyed smoked haddock

300ml milk

To serve

2 lemons, cut into wedges

coriander leaves

freshly ground black pepper

mango chutney

natural yogurt

Lunch

Smoked mackerel, fennel & chickpea salad
with horseradish & yogurt dressing

Here's a summery salad that could be served as a smart starter, too. Come wintertime, we warm it up by roasting the fennel until it's slightly frazzled and add some Slow-roasted Tomatoes (*see* page 148), too. The chickpeas can be swapped for any pulse you like, or even some couscous dressed in lemon and olive oil. Similarly, use any other salad leaves in place of the baby gem.

To make the Yogurt & Horseradish dressing, whisk all the ingredients together in a bowl.

Flake the mackerel into bite-sized pieces. Cut each lettuce half into 4 wedges.

Put the chickpeas into a bowl and mix with half the olive oil plus some salt and pepper.

Finely slice the fennel and place it in a bowl with the tomatoes and spring onions. Add the remaining olive oil, the lemon juice, extra salt and pepper and toss well.

Layer the lettuce and chickpeas in a shallow serving bowl with the dressed fennel, tomatoes and spring onions. Scatter the smoked mackerel on top and drizzle the 4 salads with half the dressing, serving the extra on the side.

SERVES 4

300g smoked mackerel fillet, skinned and boned

4 baby gem lettuce, halved

400g can chickpeas, rinsed and drained

4 tbsp olive oil

salt and pepper

1 fennel bulb, trimmed

100g cherry tomatoes, halved

bunch of spring onions, sliced

juice of ½ lemon

For the yogurt & horseradish dressing

200ml plain yogurt

40ml extra virgin olive oil

30ml lemon juice

2 tsp hot horseradish sauce

Roasted garlic & lemon thyme chicken
with tomato & sourdough salad

Chicken thighs have much more flavour than breast meat and cooking them slowly gives them a lovely soft texture, so the meat just falls apart. We have served this dish at several summer parties because it always goes down a storm. The chicken is accompanied by our version of the Tuscan salad panzanella and we always warn our guests that it is the garlic lovers' option.

Roughly chop the tomatoes and bread into 3cm cubes. Combine in a bowl. Whisk together the olive oil, vinegar, garlic and capers, season well with salt and pepper, then pour over the bread mixture. Stir well, then set aside for 3–4 hours so that the flavours meld together.

Preheat the oven to 160°C/fan 140°C/gas mark 3.

Now prepare the chicken. Combine the olive oil, garlic cloves, lemon wedges and lemon thyme in a roasting tin. Season with salt and pepper, then add the chicken and toss well to coat. Pour in the wine, cover tightly with foil and cook for 2 hours. Remove the foil and cook for a further 45 minutes, until the chicken skin is crisp.

Just before serving, toss the salad and sprinkle with the baby basil leaves. Put 2 chicken thighs on each plate, add a drizzle of the cooking juices (discard the lemons) and serve with the salad.

SERVES 6

700g plum tomatoes

300g sourdough bread, left out overnight

60ml extra virgin olive oil

30ml red wine vinegar

1 garlic clove, crushed

1 tbsp small capers, drained

salt and pepper

handful of baby basil leaves

For the chicken

4 tbsp extra virgin olive oil

6 garlic cloves, unpeeled

2 unwaxed lemons, each cut into 8 wedges

2–3 sprigs of lemon thyme

12 chicken thighs, with skin

200–300ml white wine

Chicory & radicchio salad
with roasted parsnip, blue cheese & grapes

There is nothing quite like a roasted parsnip, especially when you bring chilli and honey into the equation. This was a salad born out of the leftovers of a Sunday roast and is one of the loveliest winter salads we serve. Our preferred cheese for this is a creamy Dorset blue, which we encourage you to track down if possible. If you find blue cheese too tangy, you can substitute feta.

Preheat the oven to 200°C/fan 180°C/gas mark 6.

Place the parsnips in a roasting tin. Mix together the chilli, cinnamon and oil and drizzle over the parsnips. Roast for 25–30 minutes. When the parsnips are soft and cooked through, drizzle with the honey and roast for a further 15 minutes, until sticky, golden and crisp.

Transfer the parsnips to a bowl. Add the grapes, cheese and half the dressing. Toss well.

Divide the chicory and radiccho between 4 serving plates and top with the parsnip mixture, finishing with a scattering of walnuts. Serve with the remaining dressing on the side.

SERVES 4

1kg parsnips, peeled and quartered lengthways

1 tsp dried chilli flakes

1 tsp ground cinnamon

6 tbsp olive oil

1 tbsp clear honey

small bunch of seedless red grapes, halved

200g Dorset blue cheese, crumbled or cubed

100ml Rapeseed Oil & English Mustard Dressing (*see* page 151)

6 heads of chicory, leaves separated and cut in half lengthways

½ head of radicchio, shredded

50g walnuts , roughly chopped

Salt beef, red onion & potato salad
with anchovies & capers

We introduced meltingly tender salt beef to our menu when we opened our café in Hampstead. We slowly braise our own salt beef for hours until tender, then shred it for this wintry weekend lunch salad. The capers and anchovies add piquancy, but it's the salt beef that takes the limelight.

Preheat the oven to 200°C/fan 180°C/gas mark 6.

Put the potatoes and onions into a roasting tin. Add the oil and anchovy fillets and toss well. Roast for 30–40 minutes, until golden and soft.

Place the salt beef in a large bowl and add the potatoes, onions and parsley.

Mix the mustard powder and honey into the dressing, add the capers, then pour over the beef mixture and toss well. Taste and add salt if you wish.

SERVES 4

1kg baby potatoes, halved

3 red onions, each cut into 8 wedges

4 tbsp extra virgin olive oil

6 salted anchovy fillets, rinsed and chopped

500g Braised Salt Beef (*see* page 153), chopped or shredded

large bunch of flat-leaf parsley, leaves picked

1 tbsp English mustard powder

1 tbsp honey

200ml Rapeseed Oil & English Mustard Dressing (*see* page 151)

2 tbsp capers, drained

salt (optional)

Smoked ham, butterbean & gherkin salad
with slow-roasted tomatoes

We're huge fans of ham hock, so shredded slow-braised ham hock would naturally be our choice for this salad. Failing that, you can buy a chunk of ham and shred it yourself. When we fancy a change, we have been known to make this salad using tuna in olive oil, which is incredibly delicious as well.

Put the butter beans into a bowl and add the gherkins or cornichons, onion, parsley and dressing. Toss well.

Divide the salad between 4 plates, top with the ham and tomatoes. Serve with a good twist of black pepper.

SERVES 4

400g can butter beans, drained and rinsed

100g little gherkins or cornichons, finely chopped

1 red onion, finely sliced

large bunch of flat-leaf parsley, leaves picked

200ml Rapeseed Oil & English Mustard Dressing (*see* page 151), whisked with 1 extra tbsp English mustard powder

200g Slow-braised Ham Hock (*see* page 154) or smoked ham, pulled into chunks

12 Slow-roasted Tomatoes (*see* page 148)

freshly ground black pepper

Ham hock potato cakes
with minted peas, shallots & parsley cream

If you are not braising your own ham hock (as on page 154), you can try buying it ready-cooked and shredded; otherwise, use some finely shredded smoked ham. In summer we serve these tasty potato cakes with a combination of warmed peas, cherry tomatoes and mint in a lemon and olive oil dressing. During the winter we go instead for this easy parsley sauce spiked with good old English mustard powder.

Preheat the oven to 200°C/fan 180°C/gas mark 6.

Bake the potatoes for 45 minutes, until a skewer shows no resistance when inserted. Cut them in half, scoop the flesh into a bowl and discard the skins. Mash the potatoes, then mix with the egg, ham, capers, parsley and lots of salt and pepper.

Put the polenta into a shallow bowl. With wet hands, divide the potato mixture into 8 equal pieces and shape into patties about 2cm thick. Coat lightly in the polenta and chill until ready to use.

Place the shallots in a roasting tin, drizzle with the oil and season well. Roast for 15 minutes, until tender, then reduce the temperature to 140°C/fan 120°C/gas mark 1.

Meanwhile, place the peas, mint and butter in a saucepan, season and set aside. Put the mustard powder into another saucepan. Add a little of the cream and stir until smooth. Add the remaining cream and mix well. Set aside.

Heat 2 tablespoons of the olive oil in a large frying pan and fry the potato cakes, a few at a time, for 2–3 minutes on each side, until golden. Place on a baking sheet with the shallots and keep warm in the oven. Fry the remaining potato cakes in the same way.

Put the pan of peas over the heat and warm thoroughly. Similarly, warm the mustardy cream and stir in the parsley. When everything is ready, place 2 potato cakes on to each of 4 plates and pour the cream on top. Spoon over some peas and top with a few shallots.

SERVES 4

1kg King Edward potatoes, unpeeled

1 free-range egg

250g Slow-braised Ham Hock (*see* page 154)

3 tbsp capers

4 tbsp chopped flat-leaf parsley

salt and pepper

2 tbsp polenta, for coating

6 tbsp olive oil, for frying

For the shallots

200g shallots, halved

2–3 tbsp extra virgin olive oil

For the peas

200g frozen peas

sprig of mint

15g butter

For the parsley cream

1 tsp English mustard powder

200ml double cream

3 tbsp chopped flat-leaf parsley

Four types of puff pastry tartlet   EACH RECIPE MAKES 6

Here we have basic puff pastry cases with four different toppings, which are delicious warm or cold. These recipes offer a good way of using up leftovers, and the tarts are perfect for a light lunch or for taking on picnics. Using ready-rolled puff pastry takes out some of the elbow grease required.

Mushroom, feta & thyme

Preheat the oven to 200°C/fan 180°C/gas mark 6.

Place the mushrooms in a baking tray, drizzle with olive oil, season well and roast for 15 minutes, until tender.

Meanwhile, line a baking sheet with nonstick baking paper.

Cut the pastry into 13cm squares and place them on the prepared baking sheet. Place another baking sheet directly on top and bake for 12–15 minutes, until the squares are crisp and pale golden but not risen.

Divide the mushrooms between the pastry squares. Top each one with 15g of the feta, a drizzle of oil and a sprinkling of thyme leaves. Bake for a further 5 minutes to warm through.

6 large or 12 small Portobello mushrooms
olive oil, for drizzling
salt and pepper
300g ready-rolled frozen puff pastry, defrosted overnight
90g feta cheese, sliced
thyme leaves

Curly kale, Stilton & chilli jam

Preheat the oven to 200°C/fan 180°C/gas mark 6.

Wash the kale and place it in a saucepan with just the residual water clinging to it and heat until wilted. Drain and roughly chop.

Place some kale on each baked pastry square and top with 25g of the cheese and 2 teaspoons of chilli jam. Warm in the oven for 5 minutes.

6 baked puff pastry squares (*see* method above)
400g curly kale
150g Stilton cheese
60g chilli jam

Goats' cheese, ham & fig chutney

Preheat the oven to 200°C/fan 180°C/gas mark 6.

Spread each pastry square with 1 tablespoon of the chutney and sprinkle with 10g of the goats' cheese. Warm in the oven for 5 minutes.

Drape a slice of ham over the top and finish with a few rocket leaves and a good twist of black pepper.

6 baked puff pastry squares (*see* method opposite)

6 tbsp fig chutney

60g goats' cheese

6 slices of air-dried ham (we use British cured ham, but prosciutto, speck or Serrano ham will do)

rocket leaves, to serve

freshly ground black pepper

New potato, caramelized onion & Brie

Heat the oil in a frying pan. Add the potatoes, onion and salt, then cover and cook over a low heat for 15 minutes, stirring occasionally, until completely soft. Leave to cool in the covered pan.

Preheat the oven to 200°C/fan 180°C/gas mark 6.

Spoon the potato mixture on to the baked pastry squares, add slices of Brie to each one and warm in the oven for 5 minutes, until the cheese has melted.

Finish with a twist of black pepper, garnish with chopped parsley and serve.

3 tbsp olive oil

300g new potatoes, sliced 5mm thick

1 onion, thinly sliced

pinch of salt

6 baked puff pastry squares (*see* method opposite)

120g Brie cheese, cut into slices

freshly ground black pepper

small bunch of flat-leaf parsley, leaves picked, to garnish

Mushroom & tarragon soup
with horseradish cream

In our busy kitchens, roasting mushrooms in the oven means there's one less thing to stir on the crowded hob. At home you can, of course, cook them in a saucepan, but roasting does intensify their earthy flavour and brings out their sweetness. Adding sourdough breadcrumbs to a mushroom soup gives it a lovely depth of flavour and also prevents it from separating. If you want a gluten-free version, omit the bread and add more mushrooms to compensate.

Preheat the oven to 200°C/fan 180°C/gas mark 6.

Put the mushrooms in a large roasting tin with the oil, garlic, salt and pepper. Roast for 25–30 minutes, until tender and golden.

Meanwhile, make the horseradish cream. Mix the horseradish with the cream and lemon juice. Taste, adjust the lemon juice as necessary and season to taste. Set aside.

Transfer the mushrooms to a saucepan, add the tarragon and breadcrumbs and heat for 5 minutes. Pour in the stock and bring to a simmer.

Purée the soup and loosen with water if you feel it is a bit thick. Season well and add lemon juice to taste. Finish with the double cream.

Serve the soup in bowls and drizzle a little horseradish cream over the top.

SERVES 4–6

500g chestnut mushrooms

4 tbsp extra virgin olive oil

2 large garlic cloves, chopped

salt and pepper

2 sprigs of tarragon, finely chopped

100g sourdough breadcrumbs (made from crustless stale bread)

1 litre vegetable stock

juice of ½ lemon, or to taste

50ml double cream

For the horseradish cream

1 tbsp hot horseradish sauce or ½ tbsp grated fresh horseradish

150ml double cream

dash of lemon juice

Parsnip & chestnut soup
with mustard butter

Sweet parsnips make a really satisfying soup. They need to be slowly sweated with butter to become fluffy and caramelized, so don't rush that part of the process. We like to use chicken stock to underpin the flavour of the soup, but if you want to keep it vegetarian, use vegetable stock instead.

Place the parsnips and butter in a large saucepan, cover and cook over a very low heat for 30 minutes, stirring often, until soft and golden.

Add the chestnuts and honey and increase the heat until the chestnuts caramelize a little. Cover with the stock and simmer for a further 20 minutes, until the chestnuts are really soft and will squidge against the side of the pan when pressed with the back of a spoon.

Meanwhile, make the mustard butter. Melt the butter in a saucepan, then add the mustard and heat until it starts to smell fragrant and the seeds pop a little. Add the lemon juice and take off the heat.

Blend the soup to a purée, then return it to the pan and loosen it with a little water. Add the cream and season well with salt, pepper and lemon juice.

Divide the soup between 4–6 bowls and drizzle each serving with a little of the mustard butter.

SERVES 4–6

1.5kg parsnips, peeled and thinly sliced

50g butter

200g cooked peeled chestnuts

1 tbsp honey

1 litre chicken stock

100ml double cream

salt and pepper

juice of ½ lemon

For the mustard butter

100g butter

1 tbsp wholegrain mustard

juice of ½ lemon

Cauliflower soup
with blue cheese & chutney

When cooked for a long time, cauliflower has a beautiful velvety texture with a nutty and slightly spicy flavour. It goes excellently with blue cheese, but needs some sharpness to stop the whole thing getting too cloying, so we add lemon and a dollop of chutney as a garnish.

Place the potatoes and onion in a large saucepan. Add the thyme and butter, cover and cook over a low heat until the potato is tender and the onion, translucent. Add the garlic and cauliflower, stirring to coat in the butter, and cook for 5 minutes. Pour in the stock, cover and simmer for 30 minutes, or until the cauliflower is tender.

Blend the soup to a smooth purée, then return it to the saucepan and loosen with a little water if necessary. Add the cream and heat through. Season well and add lemon juice to taste.

Set out your soup bowls. Crumble a little blue cheese or Stilton into each one, spoon the chutney on top and pour the soup around it. Add a twist of black pepper on top and serve with slices of toasted granary bread.

SERVES 6

2 large potatoes, cubed

1 onion, diced

sprig of thyme

50g butter

2 garlic cloves, crushed

1 medium cauliflower (about 600g), trimmed and broken into 3–4cm florets

1 litre vegetable stock

200ml double cream

juice of ½ lemon

250g Dorset blue cheese or Stilton cheese

4 tbsp chutney (we use pear or apple chutney)

freshly ground black pepper

slices of toasted granary bread, to serve

Spiced butternut squash & coconut soup

Sweet roasted butternut squash and spices are a culinary match made in heaven. Adding coconut milk really enriches the soup and tempers the flavours of the spices. Play around with how much chilli you want to add, or serve with chilli oil for drizzling if you are not sure how hot other people might like it.

Preheat the oven to 220°C/fan 200°C/gas mark 7.

Halve the squash and scoop out the seeds and discard. Place the squash in a large roasting tin.

Mix the oil with the garlic, cinnamon, fennel seeds, chilli and plenty of salt and pepper. Drizzle this mixture all over the squash, then cover with foil and roast for 45 minutes until soft.

Scoop out the flesh of the squash from the skins and transfer it to a large saucepan. Cover with water, add the stock and bring to a simmer.

Blend the soup to a smooth purée, then return it to the pan and loosen it with the coconut milk. Reheat and serve in soup bowls, drizzled with double cream and sprinkled with paprika. Offer chilli oil at the table, for drizzling.

SERVES 6

2 large butternut squash

2 tbsp extra virgin olive oil

1 large garlic clove, crushed

1 tsp ground cinnamon

1 tsp fennel seeds

½ tsp crushed dried red chilli

salt and pepper

400ml vegetable stock

400g can coconut milk

To serve

double cream

paprika

chilli oil, for drizzling

Roasted squash & pearl barley salad
with pumpkin seeds & dried cranberries

This is a really filling winter salad. Roasted squash is one of our favourite ingredients, but it does need to be lightly spiced and cooked to the point where it loses its starchiness and becomes sweet. If you can't find dried cranberries, any other dried fruit will do, even some sultanas.

Preheat the oven to 220°C/fan 200°C/gas mark 7.

Put the squash into a roasting tin, sprinkle with the olive oil, cinnamon, chilli flakes and seasoning, then toss well. Roast for 15 minutes, then turn, drizzle with the honey and roast for a further 10 minutes, until sweet, caramelized and really tender, yet holding its shape.

Meanwhile, put the pearl barley into a saucepan, cover with cold water and bring to the boil. Simmer for about 35 minutes, until tender but with a little bite. Drain, allow to cool, then toss in 4 tablespoons of the dressing.

Spread the pearl barley in the bottom of a large shallow serving dish. Cover with the roasted squash, then the cranberries. Combine all the leaves and arrange them over the top. Finally, sprinkle with the pumpkin seeds and drizzle with the remaining dressing.

SERVES 4

700g butternut squash, peeled and cut into 4cm cubes

4 tbsp extra virgin olive oil

1 tsp ground cinnamon

1 tsp chilli flakes

salt and pepper

2 tbsp honey

300g pearl barley

200ml Rapeseed Oil & English Mustard Dressing (*see* page 151)

120g dried cranberries

100g baby spinach

100g rocket leaves

bunch of mint, roughly chopped

100g pumpkin seeds

Broccoli, sugarsnap & baby gem salad
with lemon-marinated feta

This salad is a perennial favourite during the summer months, when we feel all the crunchy green vegetables are doing us so much good. It is a great salad to take on picnics, but don't refrigerate it or the oil will solidify and cling to the feta, and the veggies will lose their flavour. Sugarsnap peas, served raw when in season, are sweet and crunchy, but if those you find are not at their best, you might want to blanch them quickly first. Alternatively, throw in some fresh peas straight from the pod.

Cook the broccoli in a large pan of boiling salted water for about 3 minutes, until tender but still crunchy. Drain in a colander, cool under cold running water, then shake dry.

Combine the oil and lemon zest in a bowl, then crumble in the feta.

Cut each lettuce half into 4 wedges lengthways. Place in a large bowl with the radishes, broccoli, sugarsnap peas and cucumber. Drizzle the dressing over everything and toss well.

Divide the salad between 4 bowls, placing the marinated feta on top. Finish with a good twist of black pepper.

SERVES 4

300g broccoli florets

salt and pepper

2 tbsp rapeseed oil or olive oil

finely grated zest of 1 lemon

300g feta cheese

4 baby gem lettuce, halved lengthways

8 radishes, thinly sliced

125g sugarsnap peas, halved lengthways

½ cucumber, thinly sliced

100ml Rapeseed Oil & English Mustard Dressing (*see* page 151)

Green lentil, beetroot & red onion salad
with goats' cheese

For this salad we use a non-matured British goats' cheese, which has a fresh, tart flavour and no rind, and our mustardy dressing. It works well in both summer and winter. It's important that the lentils retain some bite, so take care not to overcook them.

Preheat the oven to 200°C/fan 180°C/gas mark 6.

Put the beetroot in a saucepan of water and bring to the boil, then simmer for 30–45 minutes, until tender. Drain well, then rub off the skin and cut into quarters.

Meanwhile, cook the lentils in a pan of boiling water for 20–25 minutes, until tender but not slushy. Drain in a colander, hold under running water until cool, then drain again.

Place the lentils in a large bowl and stir in half the dressing. Add the parsley, and top with the beetroot and onion. Sprinkle the cheese over the top, add a twist of black pepper and serve with the remaining dressing on the side.

SERVES 4

9 beetroot, trimmed but unpeeled

300g green Puy lentils

200ml Rapeseed Oil & English Mustard Dressing (*see* page 151)

bunch of flat-leaf parsley, leaves picked

1 red onion, sliced

250g goats' cheese, crumbled

freshly ground black pepper

Warm red rice & chicken salad
with green beans & dates

The nutty flavour and satisfying bite of red rice make it ideal for a warm salad and we nearly always sell out of this particular one. On the rare occasions there is some left at the end of the day, there's a fight over who gets to take it home. Note that olives can be used instead of dates, and the chicken may be replaced with avocado to make the salad meat-free. Make sure you dress the rice while it's still warm so it absorbs the flavours really well.

Preheat the oven to 180°C/fan 160°C/gas mark 4.

Put the chicken in a roasting tin, drizzle with the olive oil and season generously with salt and pepper. Place in the oven and roast for 30–45 minutes. When cooked, skin and bone the chicken, then shred the meat.

Meanwhile, cook the rice in a pan of salted boiling water for 25–30 minutes, until tender. Drain in a sieve, then transfer to a bowl and toss in the dressing while still warm. Add seasoning to taste, being fairly generous with salt, then stir in the herbs.

Blanch the beans in boiling water for 3–4 minutes, until tender. Add to the rice along with the dates and shredded chicken. Scatter with flaked almonds and serve.

SERVES 4

600g chicken thighs

4 tbsp olive oil

salt and pepper

250g red rice

200ml Rapeseed Oil & English Mustard Dressing (*see* page 151)

small bunch of flat-leaf parsley, leaves picked and roughly chopped

small bunch of mint, finely chopped

200g green beans, topped

50g dates, cut into slivers

50g flaked almonds

Smoked mackerel pâté

This pâté is really easy to make – you just blend all the ingredients in the food processor – but make sure you go for a hot horseradish sauce rather than a wimpy creamed type because it supplies the kick needed to cut through the oiliness of the fish.

Put all the ingredients in a blender or food processor and blitz until smooth but not puréed – a maximum of 30 seconds, depending how good your blades are.

If serving later in the day, cover and chill, but take the pâté out of the refrigerator and allow it to come to room temperature before use.

Sprinkle the pâté with extra cayenne pepper and serve with slices of granary toast and a watercress salad.

SERVES 2

3 smoked mackerel fillets, skinned

50g crème fraîche

20g butter, softened

½ tbsp hot horseradish sauce

pinch of cayenne pepper

lemon juice, to taste

To serve

slices of granary toast

watercress salad

Smoked mackerel pâté club sandwich

Salty fish and crisp smoky bacon go beautifully together here. Note that the recipe above makes more pâté than the sandwiches require, but any leftovers are great as a snack.

Fry the bacon in the oil over a high heat until crisp. Keep warm. Toast the bread.

Take 2 slices of bread and spread each of them with 2 tablespoons of the pâté. Place 2 rashers of bacon, 2 tomatoes and some lettuce on another 2 slices and sit these slices on top of the pâté slices so you have 2 double-deckers.

Spread 1 tablespoon of mayonnaise on each slice of the remaining toast and place mayo-side down on the lettuce to make 2 triple-deckers. Cut in half diagonally and serve.

MAKES 2

4 rashers of smoked back bacon

1 tbsp sunflower oil

6 slices of granary tin loaf, thinly sliced

4 tbsp Smoked Mackerel Pâté (see above)

4 Slow-roasted Tomatoes (see page 148)

iceberg lettuce, shredded

2 tbsp mayonnaise

Macaroni cheese
with rosemary sourdough croutons

This dish can easily turn into a blobby mess if you overcook the pasta, so aim to have it just on the hard side of *al dente*. Make your white sauce slightly runnier than normal (only just coating the back of a spoon) because pasta absorbs moisture and also dries out a bit in the oven.

Preheat the oven to 220°C/fan 200°C/gas mark 7.

Cook the pasta in plenty of salted boiling water for 1–2 minutes fewer than the packet instructions, until barely *al dente*.

Meanwhile, make the cheese sauce. Melt the butter in a saucepan, add the flour and cook for 1 minute until smooth and bubbling. Take off heat and gradually add the milk, stirring until smooth, then add the cream. Return to the heat and stir until very lightly coating the back of the spoon. Take off the heat again and add the cheeses, stirring until melted. Taste and season with salt and pepper.

Drain the pasta, return it to the saucepan and stir in the sauce. Transfer to an ovenproof dish, sprinkle with the crushed croutons and bake for 6–8 minutes, until bubbling around the edges.

SERVES 4

400g dried macaroni

pinch of salt

2 handfuls of Rosemary Sourdough Croutons, crushed (*see* page 155)

For the cheese sauce

50g butter

2 tbsp plain flour

200ml milk

200ml double cream

50g Parmesan cheese, grated

50g mature Cheddar cheese or Gruyère cheese, grated

salt and pepper

Steak with Gentleman's Relish
& tarragon butter

I think we're a bit obsessed with Gentleman's Relish at Ginger & White. It's a salty little number made from anchovies and spices and we offer it on the communal tables alongside brown sauce and ketchup. When we opened in Belsize Park our first chef, Tom, came up with this magnificent butter and now we always keep some in the freezer. It's also great for slathering on roast beef sarnies.

First make the tarragon butter. Blitz the tarragon leaves in a food processor, then add the butter and Gentleman's Relish and blitz again. Roll the butter into a sausage, wrap in clingfilm and store in the refrigerator.

Place a griddle pan over a high heat until really hot. Season the steaks with salt and pepper and brush with oil. Cook for 2 minutes on each side for medium rare, or longer if you prefer your steak medium to well done. Take off the heat and leave to rest for 2 minutes.

Slice and top with a disc or two of the flavoured butter. Serve with mixed salad leaves.

SERVES 2

2 x 250g rump steaks

salt and pepper

olive oil

mixed salad leaves, to serve

For the tarragon butter

2 sprigs of tarragon, leaves only

125g butter, softened

1 tbsp Gentleman's Relish

Sarnies

Goats' curd & baby spinach on white stick
with red onion marmalade

A chunky white stick with crackled crust makes this sarnie out of this world, but granary or sourdough breads are good second bests. A very fresh citrusy goats' cheese or, even better, goats' curd works well against the sweetness of caramelized onions.

Cut the stick into 4 pieces then cut each piece in half. Butter one half of each piece, top with the goats' curd or cheese and spoon over the marmalade.

Finish with a small mound of baby spinach and a twist of black pepper. Cut in half and serve.

SERVES 4

25g butter, softened

1 large white stick

200g goats' curd or soft goats' cheese

2 tbsp red onion marmalade

20g baby spinach

freshly ground black pepper

Brie, tomato & baby basil on rye bread

We use a very malty, 100 per cent rye bread for this sandwich, which pairs beautifully with creamy Somerset Brie. Look out for delicate leaves of baby basil if you can find it, or just use torn basil leaves.

Put the tomatoes on a plate, drizzle with the oil and season with salt and pepper.

Butter the bread. Put slices of Brie on 5 pieces of the bread. Top with 2 slices of tomato and sprinkle with the basil cress. Top with the remaining bread. Cut in half and serve.

SERVES 5

2 tomatoes, each cut into 5 slices

1 tsp olive oil

salt and pepper

50g butter

10 slices of 100 per cent rye bread

300g Somerset Brie, sliced 1 cm thick

5g baby basil

Garlic & fennel slow-roasted pork baps
with apple sauce & garlic mayo

We serve these baps at Hampstead's Christmas fair and also make them for Sunday lunch throughout the winter. Meltingly tender pork meat and crispy crackling are piled inside a soft bun with lashings of tart sauce or chutney. The pork itself is also good for a dinner dish served with stir-fried kale. Any leftovers can, of course, be used to fill the baps the next day.

Preheat the oven to 150°C/fan 130°C/gas mark 2.

Turn the pork skin side down and make small slits all over the flesh. Slot the garlic into the slits, then sprinkle with chilli flakes, half the fennel seeds and the salt.

Place the joint in a deep roasting tin, skin side up, and dry the skin with kitchen paper. Smear with the oil and the remaining fennel seeds. Roast in the oven for 4 hours. If the skin does not produce good crackling, carefully slice it off and place under a medium-hot grill until it blisters. Meanwhile, pull the meat apart with 2 forks.

Spread the garlic mayo on one half of each bap; butter the other half and smear it with apple sauce. Pile some pork and crackling on the base of each bap, sandwich together and serve immediately.

MAKES 8

1.8kg pork shoulder, rolled and boned, skin scored

3 garlic cloves, thickly sliced

1 tsp chilli flakes

1 tbsp fennel seeds

1 tbsp salt

2 tbsp extra virgin olive oil

200ml Roasted Garlic Mayonnaise (*see* page 150)

8 soft white baps, cut in half

100g butter, softened

200ml Bramley Apple Sauce (*see* page 157) or rhubarb chutney

Pulled ham hock on potato sourdough
with roasted mustardy shallots

Our sandwiches are made with a lot of love and the very best of British ingredients, from artisan breads and cheeses to chutneys and free-range meats. We try very hard to devise original flavour combinations and this one was created for us by Scott, one of our chefs. Slow-braised ham hock is so different to sliced ham – it offers extra pillowy softness as well as a salty, smoky flavour. The chefs who make this sandwich often end up with yellow hands from the turmeric in the mustardy shallots.

Preheat the oven to 160°C/fan 140°C/gas mark 3.

First make the mustardy shallots. Combine the mustard seeds, turmeric and mustard powder in a roasting tin and mix in the oil. Add the shallots or small onions and toss well. Roast for 30–40 minutes, until soft but not browned, and the spices are thoroughly cooked.

Cut the loaf into quarters, slice each quarter in half and butter each half. Pile the ham on the bottom slices of each sourdough quarter, top with the shallots and sprinkle with the parsley. Top with the remaining bread and serve.

SERVES 4

| 1 potato sourdough ring |
| 50g butter, softened |
| 250g Slow-braised Ham Hock (*see* page 154), shredded |
| handful of flat-leaf parsley leaves |

For the mustardy shallots

| ½ tsp yellow mustard seeds |
| ½ tsp ground turmeric |
| 1 tsp English mustard powder |
| 2 tbsp olive oil |
| 2 large shallots or small onions, cut into wedges through the root |

Coronation chicken sandwich

To lighten the mayonnaise in the chicken mixture – a recipe originally created for the Queen's coronation in 1953 – we add some yogurt and sharp chutney. If using a korma paste that has already had its spices cooked out, you can simply stir all the ingredients together. The chicken filling is also delicious served at room temperature on hot white toast.

Put the chicken in a bowl with the yogurt, mayonnaise, korma paste and chutney and mix well. Season with salt and pepper, then taste and add the honey if the flavour is too sharp.

Butter 4 slices of the bread. Place about 4 tablespoons of the chicken mixture on each piece, then top with some of the lettuce and the other slices of bread. Cut in half and serve.

MAKES 4

375g cooked chicken, shredded

100ml plain yogurt

100ml mayonnaise

2 tbsp korma paste

2 tbsp mango or apricot and ginger chutney

salt and pepper

1 tbsp clear honey (optional)

25g butter, softened

8 slices of white bloomer bread

iceberg or baby gem lettuce, shredded

Roast chicken, bacon & caper mayo bap

A good chicken sandwich needs plenty of mayonnaise spiked with English mustard, capers and cornichons. It's a great way to use up the remains of a roast chicken, and the mayo also works really well with salami or smoked salmon sarnies.

Place the chicken in a bowl, add the caper mayonnaise and stir well.

Fry the bacon in a frying pan until crisp.

Slice the baps in half, butter them and pile the chicken mixture on one half. Add a handful of radicchio and a rasher of bacon to each. Top with the remaining bap halves and serve.

MAKES 6

600g cooked chicken, shredded

100ml Caper Mayonnaise (*see* page 150)

6 rashers of smoked back bacon

6 white baps

30g butter, softened

½ head of radicchio, leaves torn

Salt beef on sourdough
with cucumber pickles & mustard mayo

We slowly braise our own salt beef using brisket and spices to make a really tender, slightly sticky filling for this classic sarnie. It is also worth making your own cucumber pickles instead of buying them because the shop-bought ones tend to be quite acidic. If you prefer not to toast the bread (though the sandwich really is more delicious that way), omit the cheese – it somehow seems like overkill on fresh bread.

Put the mayonnaise and mustard powder into a bowl and mix together until combined.

Butter the bread slices and spread the mustard mayo on half the buttered slices. Layer the salt beef, cheese and pickles on the slices with the mayo and top with the remaining buttered bread.

Toast the sandwiches in batches in a panini grill or a medium-hot frying pan until the cheese has melted and the bread is lightly toasted. Cut in half and serve straight away, with a side of chunky chips, if desired.

MAKES 4

60g mayonnaise

1 tsp English mustard powder

40g butter, softened

8 slices of sourdough bloomer

200g Braised Salt Beef (*see* page 153), thinly sliced

60g mature Cheddar cheese, sliced

12 Cucumber Pickles (*see* page 153)

chunky chips, to serve (optional)

Chorizo & tomato in ciabatta
with caper mayo

We use a British chorizo supplier called Bath Pig for this sarnie. The caper mayo cuts though the richness of the chorizo, whilst making the chewy ciabatta deliciously moist.

Open out the loaf and butter the bottom half. Spread with the caper mayonnaise. Cover with the chorizo, tomatoes and cress, then add a twist of black pepper.

Sandwich the bread together then cut into 4 and serve.

MAKES 4

1 ciabatta or potato sourdough loaf, cut in half horizontally

25g butter, softened

80g Caper Mayonnaise (*see* page 150)

20 thin slices of chorizo

2 plum tomatoes, thinly sliced

handful of mustard cress

freshly ground black pepper

Fish finger, lettuce & tartare sauce sarnie

It seems every menu these days is offering a fish finger sarnie, but when we first opened in Hampstead this was still very much a guilty pleasure. You need fresh white squidgy bread — it cannot be a day old — and the fish fingers are very much better if deep-fried. We think the uniform frozen fish fingers you buy are better in a sarnie than homemade ones, and we're not ashamed to admit it.

Fill a deep-fat fryer with oil and heat to 180°C, or preheat the oven to 200°C/fan 180°C/gas mark 6 and put a lightly oiled roasting tin inside to heat.

Deep-fry the fish fingers for 3–4 minutes or bake them in the oven for 10–12 minutes, until golden.

Meanwhile, butter 2 slices of the bread and spread the other 2 slices with tartare sauce. Put the fish fingers and lettuce on the saucy side, cover with the remaining bread, then slice in half and serve, with a side of chunky chips, if desired.

MAKES 2

oil, for deep-frying or greasing

8 good-quality fish fingers

20g butter

4 slices of soft white bread

4 tbsp tartare sauce

1 baby gem lettuce, leaves separated

chunky chips, to serve (optional)

Baking

Savoury muffins

Arriving at work one morning, hung-over and dying for a fry-up, our first chef Jess came up with this savoury treat instead. Her first batch sold out in an hour and we've never looked back. We fill these muffins with anything and everything, although beware – using high-moisture ingredients, such as spinach or tomatoes, can make them soggy, so if you want to include them, mix them half-and-half with something drier, such as cheese or ham.

Preheat the oven to 200°C/fan 180°C/gas mark 6. Set out a 6-hole silicone muffin tray, or line a metal muffin tin with paper cases.

Place the buttermilk, or mixture of yogurt and milk, in a bowl with the oil. Mix with a fork, then whisk in the egg.

Put all the dry ingredients into another bowl and add the egg mixture, stirring well to make sure there are no dry floury pockets (it can be a bit lumpy). Don't overwork the mixture.

Fold in whatever savoury ingredients you're using, reserving some for decoration. Spoon the mixture into the holes of the muffin tray, almost to the top of each hole. Place the reserved savoury ingredients on top so you can later see what's inside the muffin. Bake for 25–30 minutes until golden brown.

Gently turn the tray upside down on a tea towel and ease out the muffins. Place them upside down on a wire rack to cool (the muffins are top heavy, so doing this prevents the lighter sponge underneath from getting squished). Turn them the right way up once cooled.

MAKES 6

| 150ml buttermilk, or 100g natural yogurt plus 50ml milk |
| 60ml extra virgin olive oil |
| 1 free-range egg |
| 200g plain flour |
| ¼ tsp bicarbonate of soda |
| 1 tsp baking powder |
| 1 tbsp caster sugar |
| ½ tsp sea salt |
| 100g savoury ingredients (see Fillings, opposite) |

FILLINGS

Marmite, Cheddar & ham muffins:
Whisk ½ tablespoon Marmite into the
batter, then fold in 50g grated mature
Cheddar and 50g chopped smoked
ham. After baking, grate another 25g
Cheddar, sprinkle a little on each
muffin and return to the oven for
2 minutes, until melted.

Tomato, feta & thyme muffins:
Add 60g chopped Slow-roasted
Tomatoes (*see* page 148) to the
batter, then fold in 40g crumbled feta
and the leaves from a sprig of thyme.
Spoon into the holes of the muffin tray,
then crumble a little extra feta over
each muffin and sprinkle with a few
thyme leaves before baking.

**Bacon, Parmesan & spring
onion muffins:**
Add 2 rashers of chopped cooked
bacon to the batter, then fold in
25g grated Parmesan cheese and
6 chopped spring onions. After baking,
sprinkle a little more grated Parmesan
on each muffin and return to the oven
for 2 minutes, until melted.

Chorizo, black olive & chilli muffins:
Fold 70g chopped chorizo, 30g
finely chopped pitted black olives
and ¼ teaspoon crushed chilli flakes
into the batter. Bake as opposite.

Gluten-free almond & pistachio cake

This is quite a modern cake for us, but it sums up our view of London. It is a melting pot of flavours and ideas – slightly Italian and a bit Middle Eastern with a G&W twist. Our interest in gluten-free cooking was kicked off when Tonia's daughter Lily Lois was diagnosed with coeliac disease. Since then, we generally try to avoid having gluten in our cakes, which is easier than you might think. We don't see why anyone should have to miss out, especially when it comes to cake!

Preheat the oven to 180°C/fan 160°C/gas mark 4. Lightly grease a 900g loaf tin and line the base with nonstick baking paper.

Put the butter and sugar into a bowl and beat together until pale and fluffy. Add the eggs a little at a time, beating in each addition until fully incorporated. Stir in all the ground nuts, the flour and lemon zest.

Spoon the mixture into the prepared tin and bake for about 45 minutes, until a skewer inserted into the centre of the cake comes out clean. Set aside to cool in the tin.

Meanwhile, make the topping. Heat the sugar and lemon juice in a saucepan. When the sugar has totally dissolved, stir in the rosewater and pistachios, then pour the mixture evenly over the cake. Leave to cool completely, then turn out of the tin, cut into slices and serve.

SERVES 8–10

250g unsalted butter, plus extra for greasing

200g caster sugar

4 free-range eggs, beaten

120g ground almonds

100g ground pistachios

50g gluten-free plain flour

finely grated zest of 2 unwaxed lemons

For the topping

60g caster sugar

juice of 2 lemons

1 drop of rosewater

60g pistachios, chopped

Orange & almond tray bake
with orange flower water syrup

This unconventional cake recipe asks you to boil whole unpeeled oranges and then simply mix them with sugar and ground almonds. This method crops up in many sources, but Tonia first discovered it in Claudia Roden's *Mediterranean Cookery*. When they met at an event, Claudia acknowledged it was in fact someone else's recipe, so it just goes to show how ideas get passed around and no one can ever truly claim ownership.

Place the oranges in a saucepan, cover with water and bring to the boil. (They will bob around on the surface, so don't worry that they are not submerged.) Simmer, uncovered, for 2 hours, until very soft and squidgy. Drain the fruit and set aside to cool.

Preheat the oven to 180°C/fan 160°C/gas mark 4. Grease the sides of a 30 × 40cm baking tin and line the base with nonstick baking paper.

Cut the oranges into quarters and remove any pips. Blitz the quarters, skin and all, in a blender or food processor until you have a smooth purée.

Whisk the eggs in a large bowl, then beat in the sugar, ground almonds and baking powder. Fold in the orange purée, then pour the mixture into the prepared tin. Bake for 35 minutes, until a skewer inserted in the centre comes out clean.

Meanwhile, make the syrup and decoration. Place the sugar and water in a saucepan over a low heat until the sugar has dissolved: do not stir. Add the orange slices and simmer for 10 minutes until soft. Remove from the syrup with a slotted spoon and dry on nonstick baking paper. Add the orange flower water to the syrup and set aside.

Allow the cake to cool in the tin, then cut into 8 squares. Drizzle with the syrup, then decorate each square with a slice of candied orange and a raspberry.

SERVES 8

2 oranges

softened butter, for greasing

6 free-range eggs

250g caster sugar

250g ground almonds

½ tsp baking powder

For the syrup & decoration

175g caster sugar

200ml water

1 orange, thinly sliced

2 drops of orange flower water

8 raspberries

Chocolate brownie bites

We find that sometimes a whole brownie is just too much, so we had a brainwave: cut them into bite-sized pieces and you've got the perfect portion (which we then eat five of). We must also mention the mini Stonehenge replica our manager Bosun creates with these tasty morsels.

Preheat the oven to 200°C/fan 180°C/gas mark 6. Line a 23cm square baking tin with nonstick baking paper, or use a 23cm silicone tray.

Place the butter and dark chocolate in a heatproof bowl set over a saucepan of simmering water over a low heat and stir until just smooth. Allow to cool.

Place the eggs and the sugar in a bowl and beat until light and creamy. Using a spatula or a large metal spoon, fold in the chocolate mixture. Sift over the flour and cocoa powder and mix to combine. Add the chocolate chunks or chips, then pour the mixture into the prepared tin or tray.

Bake for 35–40 minutes, until just set in the middle. You cannot use a skewer to test brownies for readiness as they will always be moist. They will firm up after cooling, so always err on the side of cooking them less. When cool, cut into 20 bite-sized pieces.

MAKES 20

250g butter

250g dark chocolate (at least 70 per cent cocoa solids), broken into pieces

4 free-range eggs

400g golden caster sugar

125g plain flour

90g cocoa powder

125g milk or dark chocolate, roughly chopped, or white chocolate chips

Vanilla cupcakes

It seems everywhere you look these days someone is making cupcakes, but when we first started making them in Hampstead, there was nowhere local to buy them. Some of our bakers love making them as lurid as possible (our younger clientele tend to choose these), while others prefer more pastel hues. We use a 2D nozzle to get a pretty rose effect on top.

Preheat the oven to 200°C/fan 180°C/gas mark 6. Set out 2 cupcake tins and line with paper cases.

Whisk the eggs and sugar in a bowl until pale and foamy. Sift in the flour, salt and baking powder and whisk again. Pour in the cream, melted butter and vanilla extract and whisk again.

Spoon the batter into the paper cases so that they are two-thirds full. Bake for 22–25 minutes, until a skewer inserted in the centre of one of the cakes comes out clean. The cakes should be quite pale, rather than golden. Allow to cool for 15 minutes, then transfer to a wire rack and leave until completely cooled.

Make the icing as instructed on page 156, but add the colouring and beat until evenly distributed before folding in the cream cheese.

Spoon the icing into a piping bag fitted with a 2D nozzle (*see* tip, below). Gently squeezing the bag and starting in the middle of each cake, pipe the icing in circles until the top is covered. To decorate, scatter with sprinkles or dot a few sweeties on top.

MAKES 18

4 free-range eggs

350g caster sugar

275g plain flour

¼ tsp fine salt

1 tsp baking powder

100ml double cream

125g unsalted butter, melted

1 tsp vanilla extract

sprinkles or little sweets, for decorating

For the icing

1 quantity Cream Cheese Icing (*see* page 156)

1 drop of food colouring (teeny-weeny for pastel icing; bigger for a lurid effect)

TIP

An easy way to fill a piping bag is to place it in a jug and fold about 8cm of the bag over the edge. This keeps it open and steady while you spoon in the icing.

Mini chocolate cupcakes

Delicate swirls of icing covered in little star sprinkles make these cupcakes look magical. We like to pipe it on with the same sized 2D nozzle as the larger ones (available from cake craft shops), but you can spread it with a palette knife if you prefer. To go all out on the chocolate front we may crumble a chocolate flake over them, or add chocolate shavings. Although small, they offer all the flavour of bigger cupcakes, but with just a smidgen of the naughtiness.

Preheat the oven to 200°C/fan 180°C/gas mark 6. Set out 2 mini cupcake tins and line them with paper cases.

Whisk the eggs and sugar in a bowl until pale and foamy. Sift in the flour, cocoa powder, salt and baking powder and whisk again. Pour in the cream and melted butter and whisk until just combined.

Spoon the batter into the paper cases so that they are two-thirds full. Bake for 12–15 minutes, or until a skewer inserted in the centre of one of the cakes comes out clean. Allow to cool for 15 minutes, then transfer to a wire rack and leave until completely cooled.

To make the icing, put the butter into a bowl and beat until pale and fluffy. Sift in the icing sugar and cocoa powder and beat again until smooth. Finally, fold in the cream cheese – don't overbeat the icing at this stage or it might become too soft.

Spoon the icing into a piping bag fitted with a 2D nozzle (*see* tip, opposite). Gently squeezing the bag and starting in the middle of each cake, pipe the icing in circles until the top is covered. To decorate, scatter with mini sprinkles.

MAKES 16

2 free-range eggs

175g caster sugar

110g plain flour

25g cocoa powder

2 pinches of fine salt

½ tsp baking powder

50ml double cream

65g unsalted butter, melted

mini star sprinkles

For the icing

125g unsalted butter, softened

200g icing sugar

1 tbsp cocoa powder

50g full-fat cream cheese

Mini gooseberry & elderflower sponges

A world away from the common or garden granny sponge, this is cool baking, Ginger & White style. We've swapped traditional strawberry jam for the zingy taste of gooseberry and elderflower, and we've shrunk the cakes because we believe good things come in the smallest packages.

Preheat the oven to 200°C/fan 180°C/gas mark 6 and place a shelf in the centre of it. Grease the 12 holes of a muffin tin.

Put the butter and sugar into a bowl and beat until pale and fluffy. Beat in the eggs one at a time, then add the elderflower cordial. Sift in the flour and gently fold together using a large metal spoon. The mixture should drop off the end of the spoon when tapped; if it doesn't, add enough of the milk until it does.

Spoon 2 tablespoons of the mixture into each hole of the prepared muffin tin. Bake for 10–15 minutes, until springy to the touch.

Meanwhile, make the icing. Beat the butter until pale and fluffy. Sift in the icing sugar and beat again until smooth, scraping down the sides with a spatula to make sure the mixture is thoroughly combined. Finally, fold in the cream cheese – don't overbeat the icing at this stage or it might become too soft.

Allow the cakes to cool in the trays for 5 minutes, then transfer to a wire rack and leave until completely cold.

To serve, cut each cake in half horizontally. Spread the icing on the bottom half and gooseberry jam on the top half. Sandwich together and dust with caster sugar.

MAKES 12

sunflower oil, for greasing

225g unsalted butter, softened

200g caster sugar

4 free-range eggs

4 tbsp elderflower cordial

225g self-raising flour

1–2 tbsp milk (optional)

250g gooseberry jam

caster sugar, for dusting

For the icing

100g unsalted butter, softened

185g icing sugar

40g cream cheese

Ginger & White carrot cake

We're not going to lie: it took us months to nail this recipe. The perfect carrot cake is busy, but not so packed with nuts, currants and carrot that you can't taste the delicious sponge holding it all together. And as for the luscious icing – that's why we always eat from the top down.

Preheat the oven to 180°C/fan 160°C/gas mark 4. Grease the sides of 2 × 23cm springform cake tins and line the bases with discs of nonstick baking paper.

Sift the flour, baking powder, bicarbonate of soda, cinnamon, mixed spice and salt into a large mixing bowl and stir together.

Separate 2 of the eggs. Break the 2 whole eggs into the bowl containing the separated egg yolks, add the sugar and oil and beat until combined. Stir in the carrots, then fold in the sultanas and walnuts. Lightly fold in the dry ingredients using a large metal spoon or spatula.

Whisk the egg whites until softly peaking. Fold half of them into the flour mixture, then fold in the remainder, keeping as much air as possible in the mixture.

Divide the batter evenly between the prepared tins and bake for 45 minutes in the centre of the oven. When ready, a skewer inserted into the centre of the cakes should come out clean. Allow to cool in the tin, then turn out on a wire rack and leave to cool completely.

To make the icing, put the butter into a bowl and beat until pale and fluffy. Sift in the icing sugar and beat again until smooth. Finally, beat in the cream cheese, but don't overbeat it or it might become grainy.

Using a palette knife, spread icing on one half of the cake. Sit the other half on top, then ice the sides and top. Place the walnut halves in a circle on the icing to mark out the portions.

SERVES 12

300ml sunflower oil, plus extra for greasing

300g plain flour

2 tsp baking powder

½ tsp bicarbonate of soda

1 tsp ground cinnamon

1 tsp mixed spice

¼ tsp fine salt

4 free-range eggs

450g golden caster sugar

300g carrots, grated

100g sultanas

100g walnuts, chopped, plus 12 walnut halves for decoration

For the icing

260g unsalted butter, softened

300g icing sugar

600g full-fat soft cheese

Rhubarb & almond crumble cake

Crunchy crumble, buttery sponge and tart fruit are a winning combination. We change the fruit in this cake according to the seasons, using forced rhubarb during the winter, blackberries and raspberries in the summertime, gooseberries in spring and apples in the autumn.

Preheat the oven to 180°C/fan 160°C/gas mark 4. Grease a 20cm round springform cake tin and line the base with a disc of nonstick baking paper.

Cream the butter and sugar together in a bowl until pale and fluffy. Beat in the eggs and vanilla extract a little at a time, then fold in the flour, baking powder, bicarbonate of soda and ground almonds. Beat in the sour cream or natural yogurt until the mixture drops off the spoon slowly, then pour half of it into the prepared tin. Arrange the rhubarb on top, then cover with the remaining cake mixture.

To make the crumble topping, put the flour, sugar and cinnamon into a bowl, add the butter and rub in with your fingertips until the mixture is crumbly. Add the water and the flaked almonds and mix together with a blunt knife. Scatter the lumpy mixture over the cake and bake for 50–60 minutes.

To check for readiness, insert a skewer into the centre of the cake; if it doesn't come out clean, leave to bake for a few minutes more before checking again (remember, the fruit will make it a bit wetter than a regular cake). Allow to cool in the tin for 10 minutes, then transfer to a wire rack until just warm or completely cold. Serve slices of cake, with cream drizzled over the top, if liked.

SERVES 8

225g unsalted butter, softened, plus extra for greasing

225g caster sugar

3 free-range eggs, beaten

3 tsp vanilla extract

150g plain flour

1 tsp baking powder

½ tsp bicarbonate of soda

150g ground almonds

150g sour cream or natural yogurt

300g forced rhubarb, very thinly sliced

double cream, to serve (optional)

For the crumble topping

75g plain flour

75g light muscovado sugar

½ tsp ground cinnamon

50g unsalted butter, softened

1 tbsp water

100g flaked almonds

Gluten-free lemon & raspberry loaves

Polenta adds a crunchy bite to cakes and is gluten-free. We make these cakes in mini loaf tins, but a large loaf tin can be used instead. Zigzag icing drizzled on top looks great, and, if serving immediately, fresh raspberries or strawberries give a summery twist.

Preheat the oven to 180°C/fan 160°C/gas mark 4. Grease 12 mini loaf tins, or line the base of a 900g loaf tin with nonstick baking paper.

Place the sugar, butter and lemon zest in a bowl and beat until really light and fluffy. Now beat in the eggs a little at a time. If the mixture looks curdled, add a tablespoon of the flour. Fold in the remaining flour, the polenta, ground almonds and lemon juice.

Spoon the mixture into the prepared tins and bake for 18–22 minutes, until well risen and a skewer inserted into the centre of one of them comes out clean. (If using a large tin, bake for 50 minutes and then do the skewer test.) Remove from the oven and allow to cool in the tin(s) for 15 minutes. Transfer to a wire rack and leave until completely cool.

For the lemon icing, mix the icing sugar with a drop of lemon juice and stir energetically until smooth. The icing should be thin but should hold its own weight and drizzle in nice fluid lines. We test this on a saucer first. If too thick, add more juice. Using a spoon or a plastic bag snipped at one corner, zigzag the icing over the loaves. Sprinkle with the raspberries and serve.

MAKES 12

250g unsalted butter, softened, plus extra for greasing

250g caster sugar

finely grated zest and juice of 1 lemon

4 free-range eggs, beaten

50g gluten-free self-raising flour, sifted

125g fine polenta

75g ground almonds

dried or fresh raspberries, to decorate

For the lemon icing

150g icing sugar

lemon juice

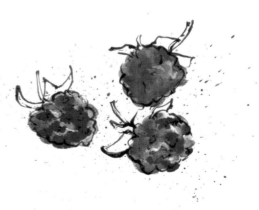

Caramel croissant bread & butter puddings

Getting the caramel really dark for this recipe requires a bit of bravery, but pays off as the sweetness is balanced by an almost burnt tang. We usually make individual bread and butter puds in silicone muffin trays, but you can just as easily put the mixture into a single large ovenproof dish. In either case, the pudding should be a little wobbly in the middle when removed from the oven because it sets as it cools.

First make the caramel. Place the sugar and the water in a saucepan and, without stirring, bring to a simmer over a low heat (stirring encourages crystals to form). When the sugar has dissolved, increase the heat and let the mixture become deep brown. Be brave and wait until it is just about to smoke and burn, then take the pan off the heat and carefully pour in the cream – this might hiss and splutter as it hits the caramel. Return the pan to the heat and stir the mixture until smooth. Set aside to cool at room temperature. When cool enough to handle, pour into a jug.

Meanwhile, make the custard. Whisk the cream, milk and eggs until combined, then strain into a jug.

Grease a 6-hole muffin tin, or use a silicone muffin tray. Place the ugly croissant ends in the holes, then arrange the neat slices on top so they protrude a bit above the tin. Pour over the caramel, reserving 100ml for later. Pour the custard over the top and place the puddings in the fridge to soak for 1 hour.

Preheat the oven to 180°C/fan 160°C/gas mark 4. Half-fill a large roasting tin with hot water. Place the muffin tray in the water and bake the muffins for 25–35 minutes, until just set in centre. Set aside to cool for 5–10 minutes. Drizzle the remaining caramel over the puddings and sprinkle with the walnuts. Lift out with a blunt knife and transfer to serving plates.

MAKES 6

softened butter, for greasing

6 croissants, cut widthways into slices 2cm thick

20g chopped toasted walnuts

For the caramel

250g granulated or caster sugar

4 tbsp water

100ml double cream

For the custard

200ml double cream

150ml milk

2 free-range eggs plus 2 yolks

Ginger & White scones

Remember to be light with your hands when making scones – it's important not to overwork the flour and butter. When it comes to stamping them out, make sure they're at least 3cm high. If not, your scones will be sad, flat little affairs, and that's no fun at all.

Preheat the oven to 220°C/fan 200°C/gas mark 7. Lightly oil a baking sheet and dust with a little flour.

Put the flour, baking powder, butter and salt into a large bowl and pulse in a food processor or rub in with your fingertips until the mixture resembles coarse breadcrumbs.

In a separate bowl, whisk the egg with only 75ml of the milk using a fork.

Fold the sugar into the flour mixture, then stir in the whisked milk mixture. The aim is to create a soft dough that's not wet or sticky. If it seems dry, trickle in a bit more milk to reach the right consistency.

Place the dough on a work surface lightly dusted with flour. Using a floured rolling pin, roll out the dough to a thickness of 3cm. Dip a 6cm cutter in a little extra flour to prevent it sticking and stamp out 5 circles, dipping again between each cut. For quirky, lopsided scones that have a certain charm of their own, twist the cutter as you stamp them out.

Reroll the offcuts – you should be able to get another 1 or 2 scones out of them. Place the scones on the prepared baking sheet and brush the tops with milk. Bake for 12–15 minutes, until lightly golden and risen. When done, they'll sound hollow when tapped. Transfer the scones to a wire rack to cool.

Serve the scones with generous amounts of clotted cream and strawberry jam.

MAKES 7

sunflower oil, for greasing

225g self-raising flour, plus extra for dusting

1 tsp baking powder

50g unsalted butter, cubed

pinch of salt

1 large free-range egg

100ml milk, plus extra for glazing

30g caster sugar

To serve

clotted cream

strawberry jam

Gluten-free marmalade loaf
with cardamom glaze

If Paddington Bear were coming to tea, this is what we'd serve him. Marmalade offers the perfect balance of sweet and tart flavours and, unlike with a lot of gluten-free cooking, this cake doesn't have a ground almond in sight, which therefore makes it suitable for those with nut allergies. We find that using a tawny Seville orange marmalade makes all the difference to the flavour.

Preheat the oven to 180°C/fan 160°C/gas mark 4. Grease a 900g loaf tin and line the base with nonstick baking paper.

To make the glaze, place all the ingredients in a pan and bring to the boil, then set the liquid aside to infuse.

Meanwhile, cream the butter and sugar together in a bowl until pale and fluffy. Beat in the orange zest and then the marmalade. Gradually beat in the eggs a little at a time, then fold in the flour.

Spoon the mixture into the prepared tin and bake for 40–55 minutes, or until the loaf is pale golden and a skewer inserted into the middle comes out clean. Remove from the oven and allow to cool in the tin for 15 minutes. When cold, lift out using a blunt knife and transfer to a wire rack.

To decorate, mix the icing sugar with a drop of orange juice and stir energetically until smooth. If too thick, add more juice.

Using a spoon or a plastic bag snipped at one corner, zigzag the icing over the loaf. Drizzle with the glaze and slice to serve.

SERVES 9

175g unsalted butter, softened, plus extra for greasing

120g caster sugar

finely grated zest of 1 orange

125g tawny Seville orange marmalade

3 free-range eggs, beaten

175g gluten-free self-raising flour

For the glaze

100g tawny Seville orange marmalade

juice of 1 orange

seeds from 6 cardamom pods

For the icing

150g icing sugar

orange juice

Lemon curd layer cake

Humour us while we get nostalgic – lemon curd on white bread is the taste of our childhood. Now that we're all grown up, this lemon curd cake is how we take a stroll down memory lane. The curd can be heated in an ordinary saucepan – there's no need to put it over a bain-marie – which makes things much quicker.

Start by making the curd filling. Put the egg yolks and sugar in a small, heavy-based saucepan and beat with a wooden spoon until smooth. Beat in the lemon zest, juice and butter, then place over a low heat for 5–10 minutes, stirring constantly until thick. Allow to cool, then cover and chill until needed.

Preheat the oven to 180°C/fan 160°C/gas mark 4. Grease 3 × 23cm loose-based sponge tins and line the bases with nonstick baking paper.

Place the sugar, butter and lemon zest in a bowl and beat until really light and fluffy. Beat in the eggs a little at a time. If the mixture looks curdled, add 1 tablespoon of the flour. Finally, fold in the remaining flour. You will be left with a really thick mixture, but don't be tempted to add any liquid.

Spoon the mixture into the prepared tins and smooth out the top. Bake for 12–15 minutes, until the sponges are shrinking away from the sides of the tins and a skewer inserted in the centre comes out clean.

Turn out the cakes on to a wire rack, peel off the paper and leave to cool. When cool, spread 1 sponge with half the lemon curd, place another sponge upside down on top and spread the remaining curd on that. Top with the final sponge, dust with icing sugar and decorate with fresh strawberries or blueberries.

SERVES 8

225g unsalted butter, softened, plus extra for greasing

225g caster sugar

finely grated zest of 2 lemons

4 free-range eggs at room temperature, beaten

225g self-raising flour

icing sugar, for dusting

strawberries or blueberries, for decoration

For the curd filling

3 large free-range egg yolks

100g caster sugar

finely grated zest of 3 lemons and 75ml lemon juice

50g unsalted butter

Stem ginger loaf
with vanilla icing

Here we have a dark, brooding mother of a cake, full of strong, spicy flavours that balance the sweetness of the icing. The little chunks of stem ginger make it stand out from the crowd, so this recipe is definitely one to impress. The high sugar content means that it is prone to getting too dark, so if you notice it becoming black after 30 minutes, turn down the oven to 160°C/fan 140°C/gas mark 3.

Preheat the oven to 180°C/fan 160°C/gas mark 4. Grease a 900g loaf tin and line the bottom with nonstick baking paper.

Put the water into a saucepan and bring to the boil. Add the butter, sugar, treacle and syrup and heat gently, stirring to combine, until just melted. Set aside to cool for 20 minutes, then stir in the chopped ginger and its syrup, followed by the eggs.

Sift together the flour, spices and salt. Add to the syrup mixture and fold together.

Spoon the batter into the prepared tin and bake for 55–60 minutes, until a skewer inserted into the centre comes out clean. Leave to cool in the tin, then loosen the sides with a palette knife, turn upside down on to a tea towel and shake once or twice to dislodge from the tin. Turn the right way up and cool on a wire rack.

Meanwhile, make the icing as instructed on page 156, but stir in the vanilla extract or vanilla bean paste at the same time as the cream cheese.

Once the cake is completely cold, use a palette knife to spread the icing thickly on top.

SERVES 9

75g butter, plus extra for greasing

125ml water

100g dark muscovado sugar

125g black treacle

125g golden syrup

75g preserved stem ginger, finely chopped, plus 1 tbsp of its syrup

2 free-range eggs, lightly beaten

180g self-raising flour

1 tsp ground allspice

1 tsp ground ginger

¼ tsp salt

For the vanilla icing

½ quantity Cream Cheese Icing (*see* page 156)

¼ tsp vanilla extract or vanilla bean paste

Gingerbread grannies

These little gingerbread biscuits sum up our attitude to family: from youngest to oldest, everyone is important. Look out for a gingerbread-lady cutter (with skirt). We like to make our grannies' hair with white icing and sometimes give them a pale blue rinse. We have even been known to add little handbags.

Preheat the oven to 180°C/fan 160°C/gas mark 4. Line 2 baking sheets with nonstick baking paper.

Place the flour, ginger, mixed spice, bicarbonate of soda and salt in a large bowl. Add the butter and pulse in a food processor or rub in with your fingertips until the mixture resembles breadcrumbs.

Put the egg, golden syrup and muscovado sugar into a separate bowl and beat until blended. Pour into the dry ingredients and mix together until a soft dough forms. Wrap in clingfilm and chill for 30 minutes.

Roll out the dough on a lightly floured surface to the thickness of a £1 coin. Using a lady-shaped 10–15cm cutter, stamp out as many grannies as you can. Transfer to the prepared baking sheets and bake for 10–12 minutes, until lightly coloured. Let the biscuits cool on the sheets.

Once cool, decorate the grannies using the icing to draw skirts, hair and glasses, coloured writing icing to mark out eyes and mouths, and silver balls for buttons.

MAKES 15

350g plain flour, plus extra for dusting
1 tbsp ground ginger
1 tsp ground mixed spice
1 tsp bicarbonate of soda
¼ tsp fine salt
125g cold unsalted butter, cubed
1 free-range egg
4 tbsp golden syrup
150g light muscovado sugar
Lemon Icing (see page 128)
coloured writing icing
edible silver balls

Gluten-free chocolate mud cake

When we first opened our café in Hampstead, baking cakes in our minuscule kitchen was impossible, so we found a wonderful local pastry chef, Alison, to bake them for us. When she moved on to open her own place, we begged her to share a few of her recipes with us in case there was a riot, and luckily she agreed. We are proud to present her wonderful 'mud' cake, which has a soft, mousse-like centre.

Preheat the oven to 180°C/fan 160°C/gas mark 4. Grease and line a 23cm springform cake tin, making sure the paper stands a little higher than the sides.

Put the butter and chocolate into a heatproof bowl set over a saucepan of gently simmering water and allow them to melt.

Meanwhile, separate the eggs into 2 large bowls. Add the cream of tartar to the whites and whisk using an electric hand whisk until soft peaks form. Set aside.

Add the sugar to the egg yolks and whisk until pale, fluffy and doubled in volume. Pour in the melted chocolate mixture and beat until fully blended.

Sift in the flour and almonds, then fold in using a large metal spoon. When fully combined, gently fold in half the egg whites. When fully incorporated, add the remaining whites and fold in thoroughly. The mixture will be very loose and runny.

Pour the mixture into the prepared tin and bake for 30–35 minutes, until well risen and the top has a wobble just in the centre. Carefully remove from the oven and allow it to cool completely and firm up a little in the tin. Transfer to a plate and dust with cocoa powder before serving.

SERVES 8

250g unsalted butter, plus extra for greasing

250g dark chocolate (at least 70 per cent cocoa solids)

6 free-range eggs

½ tsp cream of tartar

225g golden caster sugar

50g gluten-free self-raising flour

50g ground almonds

cocoa powder, for dusting

Coffee & walnut layer cake

There's something very retro about a triple layer cake. Not only do you get more of the good stuff – the creamy icing – but it looks impressive, too. Just don't skimp on the espresso. We use our house blend from Bethnal Green's Square Mile Coffee Roasters as we feel it elevates the cake to greatness.

Preheat the oven to 180°C/fan 160°C/gas mark 4. Grease 3 × 23cm springform cake tins and line the bases with nonstick baking paper.

Place the butter in a bowl and beat until pale and fluffy. Add the sugar and beat again until even paler. Add a quarter of the beaten egg and beat at full speed, then add the rest gradually, beating well after each addition. If it curdles, add 2 tablespoons of the flour and beat again.

Add the espresso and mix well. Sift in the flour and baking powder, add the chopped walnuts and fold together thoroughly.

Divide the mixture equally between the three prepared tins, place them on the middle shelf of the oven and bake for 12–15 minutes, or until a skewer inserted into the centre comes out clean.

Allow the cakes to cool in the tins for 15 minutes, then transfer to a wire rack and peel off the paper. Leave until completely cold.

Meanwhile, make the icing as instructed on page 156, but stir in the vanilla extract or vanilla bean paste and the espresso at the same time as the cream cheese. Spread it equally on the 3 sponges and sandwich them together. Decorate the top with the chopped walnuts.

SERVES 10

225g soft unsalted butter, plus extra for greasing

225g caster sugar

4 free-range eggs, beaten

3 tbsp espresso coffee

225g self-raising flour

1 tsp baking powder

75g walnuts, finely chopped, plus an extra 25g chopped walnuts, to decorate

For the icing

1 quantity Cream Cheese Icing (*see* page 156)

½ tsp vanilla extract or vanilla bean paste

2 tbsp espresso coffee

Pantry bits & bobs

Slow-roasted tomatoes

Roasting tomatoes is a crafty way of getting more flavour out of them when they're not in their peak season. We put them in a low oven with garlic, oil, salt and pepper and leave them to shrivel, but you need to keep an eye on them. If they release a lot of juice, pour it off or they will boil and disintegrate. On the other hand, you need to catch them before they get too dry. In any event, don't take them off the baking tray until they have cooled – this will help to keep them in one piece.

MAKES 750G

1 kg plum tomatoes, cut in half lengthways

5 garlic cloves

salt and pepper

5 tbsp extra virgin olive oil

Preheat the oven to 140°C/fan 120°C/ gas mark 1.

Place the tomatoes on a baking sheet with the garlic so they are all snug, season generously, drizzle with 2 tablespoons of the oil and cook for 2 hours. Check them at regular intervals, as suggested above.

Turn off the oven and leave the tomatoes inside overnight, or until the oven has cooled. They should look dehydrated, but not black.

Transfer the tomatoes to a plastic container, cover with the remaining oil and store in the refrigerator for up to 5 days.

Roasted garlic peppers

Peppers become so sweet and beautifully silky soft when you roast them – a world away from their crunchy raw beginnings. We throw these into salads and sandwiches with salty cheese and can't get enough of them.

MAKES 250G

2 red peppers
2 yellow peppers
6 tbsp olive oil
1 garlic clove, sliced
salt and pepper

Preheat the oven to 220°C/fan 200°C/ gas mark 7.

Place the whole peppers in a roasting tin and drizzle with half the oil. Roast for 45–60 minutes, until very soft and the skin has blistered. Transfer to a bowl, cover with clingfilm and set aside to cool.

When cool enough to handle, peel off the skins, then core and deseed the peppers. Cut into thick slices and place in a plastic container with the garlic. Season well with salt and pepper and cover with the remaining oil. Eat straight away, or store in the refrigerator for 4–5 days. Bring to room temperature before serving.

Caper mayonnaise

This mayo is amazing with most dishes. It goes pretty much with any fish, such as smoked salmon; it's good with salty ham or sliced chorizo (*see* page 105); and it's wonderful with bacon in a chicken bap (*see* page 100).

MAKES 250ML

1 tbsp capers

1 tbsp cornichons or homemade pickles

200ml mayonnaise

1 tsp English mustard powder

juice of ½ lemon

salt and pepper

Rinse and finely chop the capers and cornichons or pickles. Place in a bowl with the mayo, English mustard powder, lemon juice and seasoning. Mix well, then taste and adjust the seasoning as necessary.

Roasted garlic mayonnaise

Roasting garlic mellows its pungent flavour, so although a whole bulb is used in this recipe, it is nowhere near as strong as raw garlic. We use this mayo in sandwiches, such as our Portobello Mushrooms on Potato Sourdough, and Garlic & Fennel Slow-roasted Pork Baps (*see* pages 50 and 96).

MAKES 400ML

1 garlic bulb

pinch of salt

400ml mayonnaise

Preheat the oven to 200°C/fan 180°C/gas mark 6.

Wrap the garlic bulb in foil and bake for 40–50 minutes, until really soft when squeezed. Allow it to cool.

When it is cool enough to handle, separate the cloves and squeeze all the soft flesh into a small bowl. Mash with the salt, then stir in the mayonnaise.

Rapeseed oil & English mustard dressing

Our signature dressing includes British cold-pressed rapeseed oil, which gives it a vivid yellow colour. With the combination of Dijon and English mustards we find that it's punchy enough to stand up to strong flavours and perks up milder ingredients, such as lentils and pearl barley.

Combine the salt and mustards in a bowl. Add the vinegar and slowly trickle in the oils, whisking until emulsified. Alternatively, put all the ingredients in a screw-top jar and shake thoroughly rather than whisk.

MAKES 325ML

½ tsp salt
½ tbsp Dijon mustard
1 tsp English mustard powder
75ml white wine vinegar
150ml sunflower oil
100ml cold-pressed rapeseed oil

Cucumber pickles

Shop-bought gherkins can be very acidic, so making your own allows you to get the balance of sweetness and acidity just right and is also easier than you might imagine. Eat the pickles with braised salt beef (*see* right), smoked salmon or just a hunk of good cheese and crusty sourdough.

MAKES 3 X 1 LITRE JARS

3 cucumbers, sliced 5mm thick

1 onion, thinly sliced

2 tbsp sea salt

½ tsp celery seeds

½ tbsp mustard seeds

300ml white wine vinegar

150ml water

300g granulated sugar

Place the cucumber slices, onion and salt in a large, non-metallic bowl and mix well. Cover with clingfilm and chill for 2 hours. Rinse and drain well, then transfer to a clean bowl.

Sterilize your jars and lids as described on page 30. Pack the cucumbers and onion into the jars so they fit snugly.

Put the seeds, vinegar, water and sugar in a small saucepan. Bring to the boil and simmer until the sugar has dissolved. Pour the liquid over the cucumbers so they are completely covered, topping up with boiling water if necessary. Seal tightly, then label and date. The pickles will keep for at least 6 months.

Braised salt beef

Brisket is our preferred cut for making salt beef. We ask the butcher to salt it for us so all we have to do is slowly braise it until meltingly tender. We sometimes make a hash out of leftover salt beef, frying it with chopped cooked potatoes, softened onions and a handful of parsley. Otherwise, it's perfect in a sandwich, as on page 102 with cucumber pickles.

MAKES 1KG

1kg salted beef brisket

1 tbsp black peppercorns

1 tbsp coriander seeds

a few parsley stalks

200ml white wine vinegar

1 carrot, sliced

1 onion, quartered

Soak the brisket in cold water overnight to remove the excess salt, then drain well.

Crush the spices in a mortar with a pestle and rub them into the beef. Cover with clingfilm and leave overnight in the fridge.

Fill a large saucepan with water, add the parsley, vinegar, carrot and onion, then lower the beef into it and bring to the boil, skimming off any scum that rises to the top. Reduce the heat, cover with a lid and simmer for 4 hours. Alternatively, place everything in a covered casserole dish and cook in an oven preheated to 140°C/fan 120°C/gas mark 1 for 4 hours.

Slow-braised ham hock

In case you hadn't already guessed, we're passionate about all things porky. We adore a braised ham hock, which has all the texture of a slow-cooked lamb shank but the flavour of a smoky piece of ham. You don't need much of it to perk up a salad or soup and we love it piled into a sandwich, as on page 99.

Soak the ham hock in cold water overnight to remove the excess salt. Drain and rinse well.

Place the hock in a large saucepan with all the other ingredients and cover with water. Bring to the boil, then reduce the heat, cover and simmer for 6 hours. Alternatively, place everything in a covered casserole dish and cook in an oven preheated to 140°C/fan 120°C/gas mark 1 for 6 hours.

Allow the hock to cool in the liquid, then drain and peel off and discard the skin. Remove the bone and shred the meat into bite-sized pieces. Store in a plastic container and freeze until needed, or keep in the refrigerator for up to a week and use as required.

MAKES 500G

800g smoked ham hock
a few parsley stalks
70ml white wine vinegar
1 tbsp black peppercorns
1 carrot, chopped
1 onion, roughly chopped

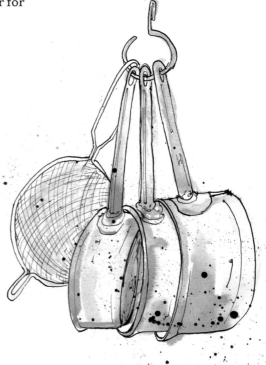

Rosemary sourdough croutons

We go through an enormous amount of sourdough bread in our cafés. Preferring the traditional bloomer shape to the more user-friendly tin loaf, we are often left with lots of little offcuts, where the bread tapers off and is too small to use in sarnies. Torn and tossed in olive oil, salt and some fragrant rosemary, these sourdough bits make the most more-ish croutons and they find their way into a lot of our dishes.

Preheat the oven to 180°C/fan 160°C/gas mark 4.

Place the bread, crusts and all, in a blender or food processor and blitz until you have chunky breadcrumbs. Transfer these to a roasting tin.

Crush the garlic into a bowl, then rub with the salt to make a paste. Finely chop the rosemary leaves and stir into the paste along with the oil.

Drizzle the flavoured oil over the breadcrumbs and mix well. Bake for 25–35 minutes, until golden. The croutons will keep in an airtight container for a week.

MAKES 500G

500g sourdough bread, roughly torn

1 garlic clove

2 tsp sea salt

sprig of rosemary, leaves only

4 tbsp extra virgin olive oil

Cream cheese icing

If you think you don't like icing or buttercream, think again. The cream cheese in our recipe adds a sour edge to the mixture to stop it becoming sickly sweet. We use this icing for decorating and filling many of our cakes, such as our Vanilla Cupcakes (*see* page 118), occasionally adding some food colouring or extra flavouring to ring the changes. If stored in a lidded plastic container, it will keep in the refrigerator for a week, but allow it to come to room temperature before attempting to spread or pipe it, or you'll find it too stiff.

Put the butter into a bowl and beat until pale and fluffy. Sift in the icing sugar and beat until smooth, scraping down the sides of the bowl with a spatula to make sure it is thoroughly combined.

Quickly fold in the cream cheese – don't overbeat or it will become too soft.

MAKES 800G

250g unsalted butter, softened

450g icing sugar

100g full-fat cream cheese

Bramley apple sauce

The tangy, juicy sauce we make for our slow-cooked, meltingly tender Garlic & Fennel Slow-roasted Pork Baps (see page 96) is made specifically with Bramley cooking apples. That's because they break down to a beautiful fluffy texture while also retaining the sharpness that makes them so good with rich meats.

Place all the ingredients in a saucepan, cover with a lid and cook over a low heat until the apples have broken down and become fluffy.

Remove the cloves before serving the sauce hot or cold. The sauce can be kept in the refrigerator for 4–5 days.

MAKES 500G

1kg Bramley apples, peeled, cored and chopped

finely grated zest of 1 lemon

25g butter

5 cloves

¼ tsp ground cinnamon

Berry & spice compote

This fruity compote has been draped over our granola and yogurt from the first day we opened our doors in Hampstead. We love the fudgy flavour that the dark muscovado sugar imparts to it.

Place all the ingredients in a saucepan, cover with a lid and cook over a low heat until the berries have started to break down but still have some shape. (You don't want something that looks like jam.)

Remove the spices before serving the compote hot or cold. The compote will keep in the refrigerator for 7 days.

MAKES 400G

500g mixed fresh or frozen berries

3 tbsp dark muscovado sugar

1 cinnamon stick

2 star anise

Index

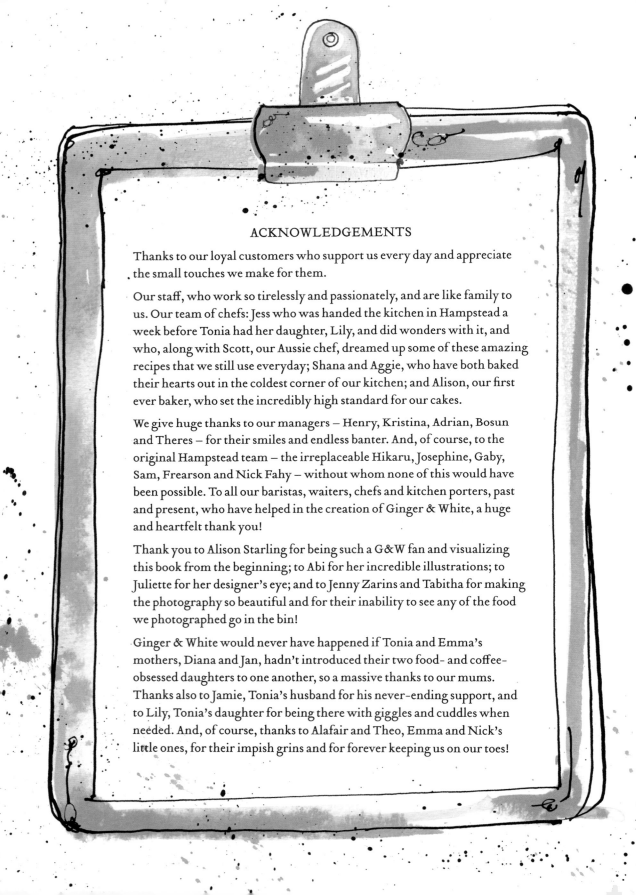

ACKNOWLEDGEMENTS

Thanks to our loyal customers who support us every day and appreciate the small touches we make for them.

Our staff, who work so tirelessly and passionately, and are like family to us. Our team of chefs: Jess who was handed the kitchen in Hampstead a week before Tonia had her daughter, Lily, and did wonders with it, and who, along with Scott, our Aussie chef, dreamed up some of these amazing recipes that we still use everyday; Shana and Aggie, who have both baked their hearts out in the coldest corner of our kitchen; and Alison, our first ever baker, who set the incredibly high standard for our cakes.

We give huge thanks to our managers – Henry, Kristina, Adrian, Bosun and Theres – for their smiles and endless banter. And, of course, to the original Hampstead team – the irreplaceable Hikaru, Josephine, Gaby, Sam, Frearson and Nick Fahy – without whom none of this would have been possible. To all our baristas, waiters, chefs and kitchen porters, past and present, who have helped in the creation of Ginger & White, a huge and heartfelt thank you!

Thank you to Alison Starling for being such a G&W fan and visualizing this book from the beginning; to Abi for her incredible illustrations; to Juliette for her designer's eye; and to Jenny Zarins and Tabitha for making the photography so beautiful and for their inability to see any of the food we photographed go in the bin!

Ginger & White would never have happened if Tonia and Emma's mothers, Diana and Jan, hadn't introduced their two food- and coffee-obsessed daughters to one another, so a massive thanks to our mums. Thanks also to Jamie, Tonia's husband for his never-ending support, and to Lily, Tonia's daughter for being there with giggles and cuddles when needed. And, of course, thanks to Alafair and Theo, Emma and Nick's little ones, for their impish grins and for forever keeping us on our toes!